Eval of Teaching

Searching for
Academic
Excellence

SEARCHING FOR ACADEMIC EXCELLENCE

Twenty Colleges and Universities on the Move and Their Leaders

J. Wade Gilley

Kenneth A. Fulmer

Sally J. Reithlingshoefer

American Council on Education   •   Macmillan Publishing Company

NEW YORK

Collier Macmillan Publishers

LONDON

Copyright © 1986 by American Council on Education and Macmillan Publishing Company,
A Division of Macmillan, Inc.

American Council on Education/Macmillan Series in Higher Education

Macmillan Publishing Company
866 Third Avenue, New York, N. Y. 10022

Collier Macmillan Canada, Inc.

Library of Congress Catalog Card Number: 85-28638

Printed in the United States of America

printing number
1   2   3   4   5   6   7   8   9   10

Library of Congress Cataloging-in-Publication Data

Gilley, J. Wade.
   Searching for academic excellence.

   (The American Council on Education/Macmillan series in
higher education)
   Bibliography: p.
   Includes index.
   1. Universities and colleges—United States.
2. Leadership.   3. College presidents—United States.
4. Universities and colleges—United States—Case
studies.   I. Fulmer, Kenneth A.   II. Reithlingshoefer,
Sally J.   III. Title.   IV. Series.
LA227.3.G55   1986   85-28638
ISBN 0-02-911830-1 (Macmillan)

Preface and
Acknowledgments

OUR MOTIVES for writing this book arose from a deep concern for higher education in America today, and for its future. The book focuses primarily on the question of where the leadership, desperately required as America and its colleges and universities move toward the twenty-first century, is to be found. It is written both for those who must seek out, attract, and support leaders who will make a difference, and for those who must lead.

America (and indeed the world) is at a critical stage of national growth, a period of economic unrest possibly unparalleled since the industrial revolution reached its zenith and began to decline some 100 years ago. Daniel Bell (1973) first began to use the term postindustrial society over a decade ago, while John Naisbitt (1982) tells us that the information age (another name for the new era) began in 1957 with the launching of Sputnik. The authors of *Global Stakes* (1982), among many others in America and abroad, have made this country painfully aware of the emerging forces of a truly international economy. Furthermore, it is now commonly recognized that the United States is an aging society, as the baby boom heads toward middle age, and will continue moving in that direction well into the next century.

Higher education is being buffeted by these and other major societal forces. Much is expected of our colleges and universities. As the number of 18-year-olds declines, and as the national defense and social security demand a greater share of national resources, colleges and universities are being subjected to intense pressure to perform better, as well as to lead the way in an age where educational excellence is critical to economic survival. However, there is no comfort, and few precedents, to be found in the conventional wisdom regarding higher education.

While growing numbers of people in America believe centrally controlled and highly regulated colleges and universities will ensure educational quality, others are not so certain. There is an invaluable bounty in the American system of individualism, initiative, and entrepreneurship that has been evident since the infancy of America. Even now, Naisbitt (1982) reports that the United States, as a nation, is becoming a bottom-up, decentralized, and individual-oriented society.

In the nineteenth century, the American higher education system was characterized by masterful, larger-than-life leaders, who left an indelible print on our higher education consciousness. The question now is, who will the new Gilmans, Eliots, and Harpers be? Who will provide the leadership required by the troubled environment in which academe must now function? What will these leaders' vision and strategies be? And, in a broader sense, what are the tactics and strategies required for institutional success today?

Those are some of the questions we had in mind in early 1984 when this grass-roots study of a special group of colleges and universities started. We found that there are important lessons to be learned and valuable insight to be gained from the successful experiences of these 20 institutions and their presidents, lessons for everyone involved in the higher education enterprise and especially for those who must assume the mantle of leadership—presidents, boards, and others.

We cannot overemphasize the fact that the 20 institutions reported on here are not presented as the 20 best colleges and universities in America or the only 20 schools "on the move." Rather they are simply 20 good and verifiable cases of schools searching for new levels of effectiveness, excellence, and/or recognition, and achieving a degree of success for their efforts. Further, it would be a mistake to generalize the findings reported in this book to all of higher education.

As we moved forward with our study, we were fortunate to receive guidance and support from many people to whom we are grateful. George W. Johnson, the president of our university, was extremely helpful, providing everything from the time to do the research to a critique of our findings; Linda Kalof, our research associate, gave us hundreds of hours of invaluable assistance in research design, field visits, and data analysis; Ted Marchese, Russell Garth, and David Bushnell all provided insight and assistance with the research and the book; Edward Taylor provided creative and editorial assistance in the writing process; the Institute for Science and Technology at George Mason, Inc., provided financial assistance through its corporate affiliates. Finally, we want to thank our associates, friends, and families who unstintingly gave us their patience and understanding during two years that we devoted to the project.

Contents

Appendices

Searching for
Academic
Excellence

PART 1
THE FINDINGS

Introduction

I find the great thing in this world is not so much where we stand as in what direction we are moving.

Goethe

This is an unparalleled opportunity for American higher education. In the best of times, colleges grow by addition. You add to what already exists. Everybody grows in the same fashion. In bad times, choices must be made, but an institution can really thrive if it has a sense of what it is doing. It's possible to shape an institution. If you look at the history of higher education in this country, the bad times have been good times for institutions with a sense of vision and with leadership.

Arthur Levine,
President, Bradford College

Much of the conventional wisdom concerning higher education in America in the 1980s seems almost designed to reinforce doubts the academy itself has about its future. The rational planners in state government, and the educational community in general, have accepted as givens conditions that can lead only to negative prognostication: The demographics of contemporary America ensure enrollment declines; providing real leadership in almost any field is becoming an impossible task; American undergraduate education is poorly organized (too many electives), and inadequate for preparing today's students to enter the twenty-first century; and teacher education schools, long alienated from the liberal arts, are in such dismal shape that half or more of all programs should be closed—among other arguments familiar to those in academe.

There is no question that colleges and universities, public and private, face one of the most challenging periods in their history. The factors engendering this crisis have been well documented. We will not duplicate the litany of causes here, but we do offer a context for reflection through the words of educational theorists and leaders.

- Experts predict that between 10 and 30% of America's 3,100 colleges and universities will close ... or merge with other institutions by 1995. (Keller, *Academic Strategy,* 1983: p. 3)
- State and campus policy makers everywhere are responding to ... declines in traditional college-age populations, fiscal uncertainty ... over-expansion ... and ... atmosphere of competition and conflict. (Godwin, *Challenges of Retrenchment,* 1981:IX)
- There is a general problem of leadership across the United States. ... There are more constraints. There is tremendous pressure ... on corporate leaders, union leaders, mayors, and so forth. But the problems and stress facing leaders in higher education may be the most intense of all. (Kerr, *AGB Reports,* 1985)

While there is something of a crisis facing higher education in America, the degree of its intensity remains to be seen; however, the facts do demand a response. What is to be done? And, equally important, who will do it?

Centralization and the Rational Planners

The thinking in many state bureaus, including state boards of education, seems to be that policies to cope with the situation must be developed and promulgated from the top. Currently, there is evidence of nation-wide interest in the use of state examinations to certify college graduates as being minimally competent in designated areas. Opinion polls indicate widespread public support for a standardized national teacher examination, an idea recently endorsed by Albert Shanker, president of the American Federation of Teachers. A January 1985 issue of the *Chronicle of Higher Education* reported movements underway in a number of states to consolidate control of higher education institutions at the state level. A prior example is the Colorado Higher Education Committee's January 1985 report to the state's general assembly. The following excerpts from this report reflect opinions across the country concerning higher education in general:

> Colorado's system of higher education is overbuilt. ... The system is badly fragmented in its organization. Its governance is confusing. The committee recommends a single state-wide governing board ... to ensure that quality is enhanced by resolving issues of role and mission ... and efficiency is enhanced by clear educational purpose.

An increasingly pervasive belief developing across the land is that *discipline must be imposed on higher education from outside its ivied walls to ensure quality.* At a time when the federal government is shifting to a posture of deregulation—rejecting responsibility for central planning and control—the states seem to be moving toward centralization.

But let us pause for a moment: Are centralization, state-mandated college missions, down-sizing, retrenchment, and the closing and merging of institutions the best ways to ensure quality, access, and efficiency in America's colleges and universities? What, if any, are the alternatives?

These questions and others mentioned earlier were on our minds in early 1984 as we began meeting informally to discuss issues in higher education and what the future might hold for both institutions and individuals.

One of the most significant things we discovered was that the centralization thrust evident in American higher education management is in conflict with successful techniques and theories guiding other segments of society and other types of institutions. For example, in their book *In Search of Excellence* (1982), Peters and Waterman discuss the rational model and how it just doesn't work in the management of the private economy. In their view, "The numerative rational approach doesn't tell us why self-generated quality control is so much more effective than inspector-generated quality control." The authors speak out "against wrong-headed analysis, analysis that is too complex to be useful, that strives to be precise (especially at the wrong time) about the inherently unknowable" (1982: p. 31).

Peters and Waterman contend that the rational model leads to "obsession with cost, not quality and value: to patching up old products rather than fooling with untidy new product development" (1982: p. 44). The question that must be asked when considering a more centrally planned and controlled system of higher education is: Who will be in charge—the rational planners, shaping through pruning and favoring the traditional and the conservative?

Peters and Waterman made a strong case against rational centralist planning and control in the business world. From another perspective John Naisbitt, in *Megatrends,* contends that the apparent trend towards centralizing higher education is contrary to general societal trends.

> Centralized structures are crumbling all across America. But our society is not falling apart. Far from it. The people of the country are rebuilding America from the bottom up into a stronger, more diverse society. The decentralization of America has transformed politics, business, our very culture.... The pull of decentralization extends far beyond politics and geography. It is structuring the transformation of social relationships and social institutions as well. (Naisbitt, 1982: p. 97).

When it comes to colleges and universities, which trend—centralization or decentralization—will prevail? While it is too early to predict just what the current flurry of analysis and prescription will bring about for higher education, we do feel that the answer to the above question may be rooted in the fundamental political structure of America. As William Carey states in "The Elegance of Choosing" (*Science,* 1984, 226: 4681):

> Ours is a system of interconnectedness rather than cohesion, but it admits light, ventilation, and improvisation. It prospers through flexibility, excellence in management, risk taking, and good luck. Choices are considered, and directions readjusted or rejected at hundreds of nodes throughout the public, proprietary, and academic systems; decisions are reached for a multitude of objectives that may, or may not , bear upon the ... goals of transient administrations.

We became interested in these questions, and realized that the answers would be of great interest to others in the higher education community, especially those entrusted with the guidance of institutions. Which way will the wind blow?

Understanding the Present

In *Megatrends,* John Naisbitt states that "the most reliable way to anticipate the future is to understand the present." By discovering what is going on among the grassroots of American colleges, higher education thinkers and planners can possibly "anticipate the future."

We decided to take Naisbitt's advice and look at what is happening at the grass-roots level, but to use the Peters and Waterman model to organize the research i.e.,—identify, study, and learn from outstanding and successful institutions. However, we were not interested in objective quantification of absolutes: We make no apologies for the subjectivity of our study. We set out to identify not the very best schools in the country, but good examples of those, regardless of size or character, that are "on-the-move": we were looking for institutions not satisfied with the status quo, those determined to improve, and ambitious concerning their position in the higher education pecking order.

Our next step was to form an advisory group to critique our ideas and methodology. This group included Theodore Marchese, vice president of the American Association for Higher Education and an executive editor of *Change;* Russell Garth, deputy director of the Fund for the Improvement of Post-Secondary Education; and David Bushnell, director of the Institute for Technology Transfer at George Mason University.

Selection of Example Institutions

In the spring of 1984 we began the search for examples of colleges and institutions "on-the-move." What we were looking for was a broad array of colleges moving toward new levels of excellence or effectiveness. We sent a letter to 30 prominent higher educators in June 1984, asking for nominations of schools they considered appropriate by our definition. The letter included a one-page description of the type of institution we were looking for. The following is excerpted from that document:

> A major land grant university announces that it can no longer remain in the middle of the pack and must strike out in a unique way for a national leadership position. At the same time, a relatively new regional university which can safely grow and serve its community instead chooses to implement a bold strategic plan in an effort to achieve distinction.
>
> A well-established liberal arts college has seen its relative position eroded over the years and is now advised to limit its scope and scale back. Instead, its leadership decides now is the time to take a chance and launch a new undertaking.
>
> These three institutions are examples of colleges and universities whose leadership is unwilling to allow the future to be defined by statistics, demographic trends, and outsiders. These colleges find the concepts of 'steady state,' 'retrenchment,' and 'survival' repugnant. They realize that while colleges must react and adapt to society, they must also initiate. They believe that change must occur not only because of necessity, but because of preference. These institutions aspire for the extraordinary; they wish to pursue new forms of excellence; they are willing to assume risk for a greater good; they are on the move.

We received in reply many nominations with encouraging comments in the margins such as: "Looks like a good project, go for it"; "I'm sure that you will find many forward-looking colleges to study"; and "An excellent project, it should be very useful." The 24 replies we received were from:

Clifford Adelman, National Institute of Education
Alexander Astin, Higher Education Research Institute
Howard R. Bowen, Claremont Graduate School
Arthur A. Chickering, Center for Study of Higher Education, Memphis State
K. Patricia Cross, Harvard Graduate School of Education
Harold Delaney, American Association of State Colleges and Universities

Elaine El-Khawas, American Council on Education

Thomas M. Freeman, State University of New York

Sven Groennings, Fund for the Improvement of Postsecondary Education

D. Kent Halstead, National Institute of Education

Katherine H. Hanson, Consortium on Financing Higher Education

Richard T. Ingram, Association of Governing Boards of Universities and Colleges

Richard W. Jonsen, Western Interstate Commission for Higher Education

George Keller, Barton-Gillet Company

Alan B. Knox, American Association for Adult and Continuing Education

Theodore Marchese, American Association for Higher Education

Lewis B. Mayhew, Stanford University School for Education

Richard M. Millard, Council for Postsecondary Accreditation

John D. Millett, Academy for Educational Development

Mark D. Musick, Southern Regional Education Board

Dale Parnell, American Association of Community and Junior Colleges

Marvin W. Peterson, University of Michigan

David Riesman, Harvard University

Carol H. Shulman, Carnegie Foundation for the Advancement of Teaching

We also talked with our Advisory Committee (Marchese, Bushnell, and Garth) plus Robert Peck, Harold Delaney, and many others about the project and the criteria for selection of finalists from the 112 nominees (see Appendix A). Using multiple citations as a criterion (all of our final 20 were nominated by more than one person), combined with strong reasons for nomination, we narrowed the list to 52. Each of these institutions was then contacted by telephone. We explained our project and requested a specific set of materials: the catalog and other recent publications, information on initiatives, copies of news clippings and recent presidential speeches, and presidential biographical data.

Forty-two institutions responded in time to be included in the study. (Several others responded too late for our purposes.) After reviewing the materials received, we selected 30 colleges and universities as candidates for field studies, with a high degree of confidence that they were good cases to examine. The institutions finally included in our study accurately represent the diversity of higher education in America. They are: Alverno College (Wisconsin), Aquinas College (Michigan), Bradford College (Massachusetts), Carnegie-Mellon University (Pennsylvania), Clayton Junior College (Georgia), College of Dupage (Illinois), George Mason University (Virginia), Kennesaw College (Georgia), Lane Community College (Oregon), Maricopa Community Colleges (Arizona), Marylhurst College for Lifelong Learning (Oregon), Northeast Missouri State University, Northern Arizona University, Queens College (North Carolina), Rensselaer Polytechnic Institute (New York), St. Norbert College (Wisconsin), University of Tulsa, University of Georgia, University of Maryland System plus the College Park Campus, and the University of Tennessee at Knoxville.

Northern Virginia Community College served as a test site for interviewing methodology, and data gathered there were used in the analysis. Like GMU, NVCC was an important part of the study.

While the institutions we selected for detailed field studies and background research are good examples of "on-the-move" institutions, there were nine other colleges and universities that could have easily been included, but were not. We did not visit these nine for a variety of reasons—time constraints, logistics, redundancy, etc.—none of which were educationally or technically substantive. Those nine dynamic insitutions are:

Stanford University
The University of Texas at Austin
The University of Wisconsin
University of North Carolina at Charlotte
High Point College
Trinity University
Miami-Dade Community College

Colorado College
Dallas County Community College

The field visits formed the crucial data gathering step in the process of evaluation, allowing a first-hand look at the internal operations of the chosen colleges. Reports brought back from field visits plus institutional reports obtained from the schools were used to write individual college profiles. Using qualitative analysis, we delineated a set of characteristics common to most of the institutions, and a separate group of common characteristics describing the presidents of these schools. Our research proceeded through the summer and fall of 1984, and the winter of 1985. The result of these endeavors are reported here.

Major Findings of This Study

1. *In the 20 institutions we visited, there was not one instance of a state coordinating board level initiative that improved quality; promoted efficiency; addressed a major societal or educational issue; encouraged an institution to seek new levels of excellence; or anticipated trends or issues.* Instead, we discovered that in the public institutions, state coordinating agencies constituted one of the most significant obstacles to innovation and change.

2. Despite the great variety in size, mission, control, and location, we found *10 characteristics that are each common to at least three-fourths of the 20 institutions.*

3. At practically all of these 20 colleges and universities, *the motivating forces* responsible for the attainment of new levels of effectiveness, excellence, and recognition were *location, adversity, and most importantly, leadership.* Leadership was in fact a strong force present in every one of the institutions.

4. We discovered, quite unexpectedly, that most of the leaders of these schools brought with them to the presidency a special quality, a unique preparation for the position, a conceptual framework on which to build their administration. That quality we labeled the *parallel perspective* and it is described in detail herein.

5. Finally, we discovered *nine emerging administrative trends among the 20 successful institutions,* practices that may be harbingers of the future in higher education. These trends are identified and discussed in Chapter 4.

The 10 common characteristics linking our 20 colleges and universities were identified by determining those present in at least 15 of the institutions. A summary of the characteristics is presented here.

TEN FUNDAMENTALS OF THE ON-THE-MOVE INSTITUTIONS

Something we defined as a *strategic mission orientation* was present at every school we examined; this was a well-defined and widely disseminated statement of intention concerning the college's commitment and future direction. While some members of a college's community may not agree with the proposed mission, it is a topic of frequent discussion, both internally and externally.

Supportive boards of trustees encourage and support leaders, promote unity of purpose within the institution, allow individual initiative, and are effective institutional agents in dealing with political bodies, potential donors, and the general public. Moving toward a new level of excellence without a supportive board is extemely difficult, even for the most determined president and the most ambitious faculty or collegiate community.

The hand on the helm, or *the president,* is perhaps the key factor in the forward movement of every institution we observed. Additionally, the importance of leadership to a school's success is a factor well recognized on all 20 campuses.

Teamwork, although present as the result of differing management approaches, is a crucial aspect of life at these institutions and represents a genuine divergence from standard functioning at the majority of higher education institutions. Putting together an effective top administrative team was one of the first priorities of these presidents when they assumed their current posts. In addition, the executive team is periodically examined, reconstitued and/or redirected. Many of these institutions on the move are characterized by lateral (across normal lines) interaction of personnel throughout the school.

Keeping an eye on the community is definitely a priority for institutions on the move. Each college's external community is defined differently, but each knows its community well and all are effective at maintaining close relations.

The idea that individuals make a difference is fundamental to the success of these 20 schools. We found these institutions not only allow individuals to exercise initiative, but encourage it. As one president said, "Anybody can get in trouble around here, but everybody knows it's almost impossible to get fired."

We found among this group an unusual degree of *commitment to the institution,* from faculty and staff alike. This commitment is expressed in pride, concern for students, and an emphasis on teaching in practically every case.

On the other hand, *these institutions,* from the highest levels of administration down, *show a concern for their faculty and students.* Faculty are encouraged to buy into the institution, through policies such as retraining instead of termination, and programmatically developing "joyful" learners.

All institutions in this study are *opportunity conscious.* For them, the future is now. This opportunity consciousness extends from the board in presidential selection, down to the individual faculty member trying to develop innovative programs.

Finally, each of these institutions has an intense commitment to *quality and excellence.* All are reaching beyond their immediate capabilities toward lofty goals that might seem unrealistic to some. However, by setting their targets high, being opportunity conscious, and working feverishly to minimize risk at each turn, they have managed to move farther than anyone expected.

PRESIDENTIAL CHARACTER

While we delineated the qualities common to institutions previously listed, we also found several traits common to the presidents of those institutions as a result of interviews with over 200 campus faculty, staff, and students. The most distinctive is a unique factor we call "a parallel perspective." Because of a specially related type of previous experience, these leaders came to the presidency of these particular institutions with a highly developed conceptual framework on which to build a plan for moving their new institution forward. Each had a unique perspective on a problem, or a situation, or a particular institution or type of institution. The following comments of Robert O'Neil to the *Richmond Times-Dispatch* concerning his appointment as president of the University of Virginia are an effective illustration of the "parallel perspective":

> When I was listening to the Board of Visitors (of the University of Virginia), I sat there thinking that the problems they were discussing were familiar, that they were very much the same as those in Wisconsin.
>
> Experience in dealing with similar issues is helpful.... You've worked through solutions and you can offer possible solutions that may not have been considered.

In addition to this unique perspective, we were able to identify several other qualities common to most of these presidents.

Perhaps the most important personal presidential quality we saw was *visionary intelligence.* These 17 men and 3 women not only have received an abundance of recognition for their intelligence, but they are widely regarded as "idea" persons. They are always searching for ideas that might be applied to some phase of their institution's operation. These leaders have specific plans for the future of their schools: some are better able to articulate them than others, but all are persistently driving their institutions forward.

A key element in the success of these leaders is their ability to *create and control their working environment.* Unlike the great number of presidents described by Clark Kerr who are overwhelmed by their office, these 20 are proactively setting their agendas, forging ahead, and as one president put it, "taking the high ground."

On-the-move institutions have leaders who not only have a concept of where their college is going, but who also seem to have a sixth sense about opportunities on a day-to-day basis. They are shrewdly *opportunity conscious:* as one put it, they open the door "before the knock is heard."

Public relations is crucial to success for any president, and it is an area of great interest to these 20 presidents. These leaders clearly define their external community. Upon assuming the presidency, they take every opportunity to speak to outside groups, discerning the community power structure and taking advantage of it, and creating a particular image for themselves and their institutions that is consistent with their plan for the future. External relations are a team affair for these men and women, and they make full use of the resources of their administration and faculty.

We found that these presidents for the most part are *accessible and visible* on campus, constantly looking for information in formal and informal ways. They are willing to listen, to have their ideas challenged, and even to be proven wrong.

These leaders are *good at delegating,* but not necessarily straight up and down the organizational chart. When things need to be done fast, to solve a pressing problem or take advantage of an opportunity, they simply cut across the lines of command and go outside the formal administrative routes of functioning to get the right person or persons involved. Yet, they are able to accomplish this without eroding the respect or authority their principal assistants enjoy.

These 20 presidents are *not* in actuality great *risk takers,* but they encourage faculty and staff to take risks in order to get things done or achieve an objective. They encourage the perception that they themselves are gamblers.

Finally, these men and women are, above all, recognized as being *compassionate.* They care for their faculty and students, and demonstrate this compassion in concrete ways.

DRIVING FORCES

From the beginning, we were interested in the motivating forces fueling the drive of these 20 institutions. As a result of our analysis, we concluded that *adversity, location,* and *leadership* were the key factors. The presence of strong leadership was paramount; but the two other factors were also powerful forces.

Many of the private institutions in our group experienced crises of adversity and leadership in the late 1960s and early 1970s. Like many colleges during that period, they experienced declining enrollments, financial difficulties and the stressful transition from a leadership style appropriate for an earlier era to one required for the 1970s and 1980s. In many of these cases, specific geographical location contributed to the adversity schools experienced.

However, in other cases, location was an advantage instead of a weight pulling an institution down. Several of the colleges in our study had actually made bold moves merely to keep pace with a growing local community. Although a positive rather than negative influence, the locations of such institutions dictated that maintaining the status quo meant losing ground, as community growth was dramatic.

Moving forward was not always easy for these schools. In every institution there is inertia, a basic resistance to change. This inertia is expressed at times in the difficulty of getting diverse and often competing power blocks—faculty, boards, and the external community—to work together toward a common goal. At other times, a single constituency can be an obstacle—a faculty wary of the possibility of using limited resources for new endeavors. The tendency to look back or to look inward is always present; therefore, institutional leaders must be careful not to be worn down by these internal forces.

Public institutions in our study faced another major obstacle—the state bureaus, including the higher education board. Ever the rational planners, these coordinating boards frequently carry on a type of "war of attrition." They seem to work on the theory that only the best programs can survive a great number of hurdles. Thus, for an institution to be moving toward new levels of excellence and effectiveness, it must have a well-articulated strategic plan, initiative, teamwork, a supportive board and, above all, real leadership. But it must also have staying power—perseverance over the long haul. The institutions in our study have all these traits and more. Their experiences and characteristics are delineated in the chapters ahead.

Further, through our experiences with these successful institutions, we arrived at methodologies for assessing movement, initiating new thrusts, and selecting the right leader. We also report "How To" advice of these successful presidents on many subjects. We also can learn from the nine emerging administrative practices or trends evident in these 20 successful colleges and universities. Those nine are: the use of initiatives as a strategic management tool; the growing importance of the admissions/marketing officer, the fund raiser, and the computer czar; innovation from the bottom-up rather than top down; and obsession with image; the exploitation of alternative financial resources; new approaches to administrative structures; an intensifying focus on quality; increasing use of strategic planning; and new relationships between institutions of higher education and business. These are described in detail in Chapter 4.

We began this study in effect to satisfy our own curiosity about the current state of higher education and to find out whether the predictions and analyses characterizing the future of American colleges and universities were true. What we found, as we visited campuses, talked with faculty, staff, and students, and researched these institutions, was that many of the assumptions with which we began were incorrect. As these hypotheses basically represented the conventions of thought concerning higher education today, we realized that along with ourselves, many others in the field had a mistaken and distorted picture of what is occurring on campuses today, as well as the possibilities for tomorrow. While we make no claims about writing a definitive study, we do feel there is news to be transmitted.

While our report may be considered too upbeat by some, the optimism, we feel, is justified. Exciting things are happening in curricular reform, in resource development, in exploring the worlds of new student cohorts, and in the changing definitions of education. It is our hope that the observations and ideas we have collected from these 20 special insititutions will be helpful to any interested parties, but especially to presidents, boards, and administrators—who may be looking for the ideas and guidance suggested by the example of these successful schools, or simply looking for a little good news.

CHAPTER 1

Institutional Qualities — The Soul of a College on the Move

"MISSION": what images does that word imply? One might infer among other things zeal, and a self-created destiny exceeding mere purpose, a destiny pursued with zest and determination. Burton Clark (1970) asserts that "All colleges have roles, but only some have missions." The presence of a genuine mission was perhaps the key organizing and motivating factor present at every institution we visited in our field studies. The mission is tellingly described by an administrator at Marylhurst as "one of the things that makes a college work these days ... we are always measuring everything against our mission." *Such a fundamental force powering colleges on the move we have labeled a "strategic mission orientation."* Although this orientation takes shape in ways as varied as the campuses of the country themselves, it is not what most schools delineate by such things as the mission statement found in their catalog. "Strategic mission orientation" resembles George Keller's (1983) characterization of an academic strategic plan, and is similar to the mission orientation Peck (1983) found in 20 successful small colleges. In this study we have used "strategic mission orientation" to represent a more proactive aspect of college administration than Keller or Peck describe.

Keller defines academic strategy by exclusion, but also positively indentifies six distinguishing features of such a strategy. Academic strategic decision making, according to Keller, is an aggressive attitude about an institution's current character and its future

19

identity in a changing competitive environment. Such strategy emphasizes participatory decision making and focuses on the fate of the insitution as a whole, above all other concerns.

Peck (1983: p.3) describes the mission orientation he found at the colleges he visited as "almost an overstatement" of what each school is actually doing. Mission orientation has two elements in Peck's analysis—substance, and commitment, with institutional consensus on both of prime importance to the successful implementation of a guiding philosophy.

Blueprint and Manifesto—Strategic Mission Orientation

What we found in these 20 schools searching for excellence was that each had made, as an element of official policy, a written mission statement outlining the school's direction and its anticipated future. Furthermore, at each college or university the following are true: the mission statement is well known, and is the subject of considerable continuing discussion. The future academic character of the school is delineated in this document and the school's ambitions are clearly stated. The document addresses contemporary issues and concerns and cultivates external support for the school; but, above all else, it takes a stand on the importance of quality, plainly showing that if its stated goals are achieved, the students themselves will reap the greatest benefits.

In analyzing the phenomenon of this statement of mission among this select group, three categories of intention were identified which characterized the orientation of the various schools: Single Focus, Multiple Focus, and Broad Focus. A representative sampling of the 20 institutions follows. (For more complete details about the individual institutions, see Part II.)

SINGLE FOCUS—THE TRUE BELIEVERS

Institutions in this category have one clear and well-defined aim that shapes their academic program. Every faculty member and every student is governed by this goal, and there is an almost single-minded dedication to the pursuit of this objective throughout the college.

At Bradford College, for example, the Bradford Plan for Practical Liberal Arts is the *primum mobile* for the entire school. Every student at Bradford, and the entire faculty are involved in this curricular innovation. The plan drives student recruiting, institutional fund raising, and public relations; it has instilled a sense of pride in a school battered by poor morale, faculty dissension, declining enrollments, and possible bankruptcy only a few years ago.

Northeast Missouri State University, with 7,000 full-time students, is 12 times the size of 500-student Bradford, but it too has a single, well-defined mission focus: value-added education. The university, led by President Charles McClain, is determined in its implementation of this program to provide what the school hopes will be the best liberal arts education a student can receive at an American public university. Value-added education at Northeast Missouri drives curriculum development, the budget process, communications, and resource development, and has brought national attention to a former state teachers college located in rural Missouri.

Clayton Junior College in Morrow, Georgia, is attempting to create both "a performance and a place," in the terms Burton Clark used in his expanded definition of mission. Faculty at Clayton are seeking to devise a coherent, unified general education program that develops generic skills, and are working to integrate this into a framework within which an individual is better able to approach both life and learning. The foundation of this program, the faculty has determined, is clearly defined outcomes providing the focus for curriculum and instruction, and valid procedures for assessing those outcomes. The Southern Association of Colleges and Schools (SACS) has accepted Clayton's ongoing study of general education in lieu of the traditional self-study. A SACS administrator commented, "Our new emphasis in the standards is on outcomes ... this is just what Clayton is doing. Their approach is sound and solid, and their president is providing careful, thoughtful, impressive leadership."

MULTIPLE FOCUS—TARGET AREAS

In this category are those institutions that have developed several clearly defined thrusts which, because of geographical location, institutional history, or the surrounding community, are particularly appropriate. In these cases most faculty and students are associated either directly or indirectly with one or more of the college's areas of emphasis.

At George Mason University, the strategic mission has been defined in terms of four target areas—high quality undergraduate liberal arts, the partnership of education and high technology, the fine and performing arts, and policy sciences at the professional and graduate levels.

The rationale for these choices is simple. Because it was founded as an undergraduate branch of the School of Arts and Sciences of the University of Virginia, and as a result of the national attention currently being focused on undergraduate education, high quality undergraduate liberal arts education is seen as an imperative for the healthy future of George Mason. The school's location, 20 minutes from Washington, D.C., makes the policy sciences seem a natural subject on which to focus. As the surrounding business community consists of 800 high technology firms employing over 100,000 people, information technology and engineering are of obvious importance in building state and local political and financial support. Furthermore, as it is the only university, public or private, in a rapidly developing section of Virginia with over 1.2 million people, George Mason is becoming a regional cultural center.

The four-pronged mission orientation of George Mason has provided an overarching philosophy allowing a broad array of faculty and students to apply their talents at the school, and at the same time has established a policy that is easily understood by many internal and external constituents.

At Queens College in Charlotte, North Carolina, President Billy Wireman is concerned with the societal issues confronting higher education. Those issues he considers most pressing are: "the aging society," the technological revolution, the increasing trend toward "careerism," and the perception that college education has lost a lot of its integrity. Wireman believes that "the task of colleges and universities in this day and time is to put into a conceptual framework the pressures that are coming to bear and then formulate a vision of a particular college's niche."

Queens College has maintained its liberal arts core in the College of Arts and Sciences, the traditional part of the school, and is strengthening it by combining the core with career preparation. At the same time, Queens has responded to an aging society by moving into the adult education market with such credit ventures as "New College" and the Graduate School and with such noncredit programs as the Queens Institute of Lifelong Learning (QUILL).

At Rensselaer Polytechnic Institute, President George Low and his staff created a rallying point for the school's climb to recognition as a national institution, but they did this with several goals, all tied to a specialized traditional mission. Rensselaer's strategic focus is well understood and accepted by students, faculty, and the external community. The strategic mission orientation provides opportunities for institutional and departmental development, renews the institution's pride, attracts national attention, increases support from industry and government, and creates hopeful predictions for the school's future.

BROAD FOCUS—MANDATED DIVERSITY

Each college in this category has a mandate to serve a diverse community by providing a multitude of programs, but has managed to build its activities around a clearly formed central mission. At the University of Maryland, with its state-wide land-grant mission, the officially declared aim of becoming one of the top 10 public universities in the country is direct but at the same time includes a range of emphases. Maryland's mission provides unlimited freedom for faculty, departments, schools, and campuses to aid the university in meeting the challenge of its future. Each of the four campuses has a unique mission as a part of the university's scheme to serve the entire state with the highest quality programs possible. In addition, Maryland's University College delivers continuing education programs not only all across the state but world wide as well.

Further, Lee Davidson, chair of the electrical engineering department at Maryland's College Park campus, states that he has a genuine feeling of freedom, and the latitude to develop the department at his discretion in support of the system's strategic mission of excellence. He routinely takes the leadership in striking million dollar research or contributing deals with corporations and federal research agencies.

John Slaughter, chancellor of the primarily residential College Park campus (the flagship branch of the system), articulates a clear and specific role for his campus that supports system president John Toll's vision of Maryland's evolution. The system's branches in Baltimore and on the state's eastern shore, also seem determined to do their parts in implementing Toll's plans. Maryland's institutional aims are understood on each campus, giving the university specific benchmarks for success and providing concrete goals at the system-wide, campus, and department levels.

At Carnegie-Mellon, the current strategic mission was broadly focused in that President Cyert was looking for initiative at the departmental level to focus on creating distinctive programs. Departments were first asked to draft plans for achieving excellence on a national scale, and the best of these were encouraged and supported. Since this strategy was begun Carnegie-Mellon has been, as one person familiar with the situation told us, "on a roll" and spotting opportunities on the horizon has become a well-practiced art by everyone from Cyert to individual faculty.

The University of Georgia, the acme of Georgia's 33 school system, is the state's oldest, most comprehensive, and most diversified educational institution. In 1985 the university celebrated its bicentennial; the school's theme for its 200th birthday was "To Teach, To Inquire, To Serve." The impact of the university in those three traditional broadly focused mission areas is enormous, not only throughout the state but far beyond its borders. In two disciplines in which the school is currently concentrating its efforts "To Inquire," the University of Georgia is among the nation's leaders: biotechnology and super-computer research. In fact, by 1985, thanks to the presence of a Cyber 205 (one of only three such computers on American campuses) and a Cyberplus supercomputer, the University of Georgia will have the largest computing capacity of any university computer site in America. President Davison explains that this tremendous computer capacity "gives Georgia the ability to ask and answer the big questions that affect individuals, states, and nations."

Leadership—The Cornerstone

A crucial component in the successful development and implementation of a strategic mission is leadership. Recognition of the importance of quality leadership, and of its necessity for institutional growth, was evident without exception at the schools we visited.

While many on the campuses gave kudos to faculty, deans, vice presidents, and others, the primary credit for institutional achievement was given to presidents as those who made a significant difference.

President Billy Wireman of Queens College repeatedly told us of his "fine team" and of their critical importance to his strategic plan. Others at Queens, when interviewed, said, "Yes, that is true, but it couldn't have been done without the president." Henry Bungay III, a distinguished professor at Rensselaer Polytechnic Institute (RPI), summed up the prevailing opinion at RPI: "George Low was not an academic—but he just did a fantastic job as president." All administrators interviewed at Georgia agreed that President Davidson has confidence in the deans but they (the deans) are quick to return the favor.

At Northern Arizona University, Eugene Hughes is highly respected and is an obvious driving force on the campus. Interviews with staff and faculty resulted in statements about the president such as "He makes life worthwhile," and "He is a natural leader if ever I saw one." Alverno College's president Sister Joel Read is a dynamic and assertive leader, and everyone at the college recognizes the force of her leadership. Read is highly respected throughout the college and much admired for her managerial abilities though some people feel that she is too driving, compulsive.

Likewise, not every faculty member at Aquinas loves Norbert Hruby. Although almost everyone interviewed commented on his creativity, he was described by some as autocratic, strong-willed, and a "difficult personality." However, without exception, Hruby was recognized as having been exactly what Aquinas needed at the time he became president. One administrator observed, "He came here with the sense that there was the potential for continuing education, and he had the background and the experience to address that issue. It added a new dimension to the college." Another senior faculty member commented, "I am usually on the opposite side of an issue from him, but his personal integrity, his loyalty to the church, the college, the liberal arts, and to education in general are unquestionable. He has truly been a driving force of this institution, and we, literally, would not be here today as a college if it were not for him."

The Dominican Sisters at Aquinas interviewed by our team appear genuinely to appreciate Hruby. They recognize that he is sometimes controversial, and while they, as individuals, do not always agree with him, they unanimously praise his dedication. One of the sisters observed, "Norbert Hruby never does anything to enhance himself personally. What he does is for the good of the school."

Sister Veronica Baxter, former president of Marylhurst College, has been described as "a builder (not a maintainer); a change agent." Her successor, Nancy Wilgenbusch, praises Baxter's zeal, a trait mentioned by many of those people we interviewed at Marylhurst. A senior faculty member describes Baxter as someone who "came with a sense of mission and direction." Another faculty member observed that "there were times when things were so bad that I think it was only her faith that pulled us through. She *willed* this college to survive, and it did. Actually, it did a lot more than just survive."

During the course of our study, we interviewed some 300 people—community leaders, national higher education professionals, university presidents, deans, faculty, and students—and all emphasized the key role presidents have played in the growth of the schools we examined. This general consensus is in stark contrast to the findings of Clark Kerr in his recent Association of Governing Boards-sponsored study (1985).

Kerr found that boards of control have the biggest influence in determining whether or not presidents are effective leaders. His study states that boards, along with students, faculty, the media, and federal, state, and local governments, frequently combine to create a toxic general environment for leadership. By Kerr's estimation, around 50% of all presidents are prevented from effective leadership. However, this was most definitely not true among our sample of 20 schools. What follows are several examples of why this is so.

The Board: The Foundation

At these 20 institutions, boards were not perceived by the presidents to be an obstacle; in fact, in most cases dynamically supportive boards were an important factor in a school's perceived success, and evidence of such helpful governance was substantial.

There were three types of boards extant among our subjects, and the board type determined the role each group played in guiding the institution.

BOARD FUNCTIONING—FROM STATE SYSTEM TO PRIVATE COLLEGE

We looked at six institutions that were individual campuses in state governing board systems: Clayton Jr. College, the University of Georgia, Northern Arizona State University, the University of Tennessee at Knoxville, and Kennesaw College (plus Northern Virginia Community College, our pilot institution). In two cases, our review focused on an entire system and a system-wide board: these were the University of Maryland state-wide system and the Maricopa County Community College District. At the other schools reviewed there was a single campus with its own board of trustees: the College of DuPage, Carnegie-Mellon University, George Mason University, Bradford College, Queens College, Rensselaer Polytechnic Institute, Lane Community College, Marylhurst College, Northeast Missouri State University, St. Norbert College, Aquinas College, Alverno College, and the University of Tulsa.

In all the schools, regardless of board type, presidents and chancellors were given substantial latitude by their boards, or they were at least given forceful backing. Even in those cases where boards were not active supporters of a particular strategic mission, the presidents involved felt that their trustees both supported the idea of a strong executive and provided the environment necessary for efficient presidential functioning.

Maryland's system president John Toll was emphatic about the importance of a stable and supportive state-wide board. Toll's board is an established institution in itself, with an identity, a tradition, and a deep commitment to building a first-rate university.

At DuPage, which serves a large and sophisticated suburban Chicago county, the board is drawn from among the leaders of the community and focuses on serving the area's postsecondary educational needs. The board is supportive of any undertaking consistent with this function. Indeed, some people interviewed at DuPage cited the willingness of the trustees to support institutional advancement as a major force driving the college.

Lane Community College began with a commitment to innovate: From the inception of the college, Lane's board has supported the college in its efforts, to search for new and better ways to follow its mission. At the University of Tulsa, the board supports the college both financially and managerially. Those who work with the board say its members help cut red tape and are "a real blessing," adding that "the board is responsible and understands risk taking: They give us freedom."

At several schools, such as Renesselaer Polytechnic Institute, where George Low had served as a trustee prior to assuming the presidency, the chief executive is viewed as the board's leader as well as the institution's leader. This is certainly the case at Aquinas, where the entire current board has been appointed since Norbert Hruby assumed the presidency. Several administrators at Aquinas commented on how effectively Hruby interacts with the board. Bradford College's president Art Levine has revitalized the board of trustees. They were demoralized with the possibility of retrenchment, and Levine's successful innovations have provided them with a new sense of direction and purpose.

For the campuses in our study governed by a system board, there is considerable freedom within broad guidelines for institutional advancement. At the University of Tennessee at Knoxville the system board is not intrusive, and administrators say the board presents no obstacles to effective leadership.

Teamwork—Getting Into the End Zone

We found that the efficient and harmonious functioning of an administration is an important corollary to the guiding of a college toward strategic goals. At all of our colleges on the move we found a significant emphasis on teamwork and the creation of strong administrative teams. The successful college presidents in our study seem to ensure this, building their own teams from the top down. This seems to be a rarity in higher education, and one of the unique characteristics of our institutions on the move.

Teamwork manifests itself in different ways, varying from institution to institution as a function of both college size and mission. There seem to be two varieties of team dynamics in operation among schools on the move. In one, the team consists of individuals with complementary backgrounds, and personalities who work harmoniously, but with a team relationship that is not intense. In the other instance, administrative groups have intense daily interaction, are fully involved with each other professionally, and, to some extent, might be capable of filling in for one another. In either of these cases, teamwork may be confined to the president's cabinet, but at most of the institutions in this study the team concept permeates all administrative hierarchies. For example, collegiate deans may have their chief assistants serving as team leaders, or department heads and groups of faculty may act as teams, each with a team leader. The authority of the team leader seems to diminish proportionally with organizational rank, but the team spirit is apparent at all levels.

In contrast, at other institutions teamwork characterized by crossboundary interaction of personnel is present throughout the school. Northeast Missouri State University's highest levels of administration are sparsely populated for such a large institution: The administrative capstone of the school consists of the president, a vice president, and three deans. However, the value-added program is specifically designed to be carried on the shoulders of faculty teams, which develop courses, design tests, and implement ideas.

Kennesaw president Betty Siegel says her school has pursued a contemporary management philosophy that has emphasized teamwork. "We believe in productivity through people and have found a wealth of untapped potential in our deans, department heads, and faculty." Siegel cites teamwork as a major theme of her administration. Each meeting of the faculty during Siegel's first year focused on one theme which the faculty debated, attempting to determine what was being done well and what was not being done well. Following these meetings, groups of 8 to 10 faculty members met to discuss the issues in more specific terms. Two of the college's major ventures, the Center for Excellence in Teaching and Learning and the Counseling, Advising, and Placement (CAPS) Center, are direct results of the team planning concept. The chair of the curriculum and instruction department says "The faculty of C & I is strong academically.... More importantly, we see ourselves as a team and work as a team."

President Paschal Twyman at the University of Tulsa delegates substantially to his provost and vice presidents, and deans at the school are active policy makers. Twyman gives the staff freedom to act, but keeps certain things such as image making and fund raising under his own control. A collegial decision-making process is evident at this school, and in addition to the other factors conducive to the team mentality, the provost and vice presidents are close friends. The staff is compatible and forthright; they have the ability to work out differences with each other and with the president. A typical quote from staff members about Twyman is "I can ask anything."

At the Maricopa colleges, management is highly participatory: employees at all levels provide ideas to which policy makers listen seriously. Chancellor Elsner is accessible and fosters a casual atmosphere, with open communication and good collegial support. Those associated with Elsner say such things as "best relations I've ever had with a boss."

Alverno College is a prime example of the teamwork approach. All faculty are heavily involved in every aspect of the college, and authority is diffused among many people. There is a high spirit of collaboration at Alverno, and the college functions substantially on consensus. They hold periodic retreats during which they assess literally every aspect of the college environment, reacting to and critiquing each other, their policies, their curriculum, and their assessment mechanisms.

At St. Norbert College, teamwork was the most instrumental element in obtaining consensus for president Neil Webb's "Group Goals" program. Everyone got involved, collaboration was the order of the day, and there was good faculty-administration interaction. As a result, faculty morale is high and optimism concerning the future of the college is the order of the day.

The outcome-focused, assessment-based general education project in which Clayton Jr. College is involved appears to have engaged everyone, and many division directors and faculty members belong to the "Outcome Councils." These interdisciplinary councils are organized by theme (i.e., communications, critical thinking, value perspective). Attempting to determine what students should learn is often frustrating, but as one faculty member said, "We are all in this together . . . and that includes our president who is right in there with us."

Putting Down Roots—The Local and National Communities

A distinct community orientation is part of the strategic mission of each of the 20 colleges in this study. However, "community" is by no means a uniform concept for every campus, and the character of each institution's community varies widely. At schools like Lane Community College, the Maricopa campuses, Clayton Jr. College, and DuPage, the relevant external community is a rather carefully designed service region, usually within a 30-mile radius of the school. Land grant universities, on the other hand, concentrate on serving a state-wide community within a national context, while a private institution's community is a unique melding of local concerns and a nation-wide constituency.

The community colleges in the study were uniformly concerned with the postsecondary educational needs in their immediate geographical areas. Typically, these institutions receive political and financial support based on how effectively they meet the needs of their areas. Harold McAninch of DuPage told us, "Our board reflects the highly educated, sophisticated community we serve, and they intend for the college to be up to the expectations of DuPage County citizens."

The Maricopa schools are community colleges of true community purpose. Administration policy makers listen to the citizens of the surrounding region, and have responded with a broad range of community outreach programs.

Nowhere were the concerns of the community more evident that at Lane Community College. When the Oregon state legislature created the community college system in 1959, it *required* that there be a grass-roots need for a college before any ground could be broken. No state body or official could impose a community college on any area. The demand had to come from the citizenry. Today, the needs of "the people" are still the basis for all program decisions at Lane.

Harry Downs, president of Clayton Junior College asserts,

> You need to be trying to do those things as an institution that have a positive impact on the community ... you can become part of the community and try to help it move in the right direction by working with different community groups. If through your continuing education programs, you can bring to the people the kind of programs that encourage, inspire, improve, and educate them, then that's what you're supposed to be doing. Where the community is concerned, all you really need is an audience, an instructor, and a place, combined with the desire and the ability to respond quickly to the expressed needs of the community.

Downs views the college as an agent for change and believes that "the principal way we change is through our programs. We change people who change the community." One example of this type of community involvement is "Leadership Clayton," a program for leadership development, cosponsored by the Clayton County Chamber of Commerce and the college. During the nine months they are enrolled, individuals in Leadership Clayton develop and strengthen their skills in public relations, parliamentary procedure, and public speaking. This unique program benefits individuals by enhancing their personal and professional growth, and benefits the community by producing better informed and more involved citizens.

The University of Tulsa was originally chartered to serve the needs of the Tulsa area, with its primary emphasis being the fields of petroleum engineering and geology around which the region revolved. The School of Business is closely attuned to local business, and among other things provides an information retrieval system for the corporate community.

At Northern Arizona University, the surrounding community includes a large Native American population which the university considers a unique part of its community. The university has implemented several programs specifically designed for this special constituency, including tutoring centers in mathematics, the sciences, and education on the local Navaho and Hopi reservations.

Community involvement is a major focus at DuPage, where the Business and Professional Institute is heavily involved with the local business community. Among other projects, the college operates a radio station as an outreach arm to those who cannot, or choose not to, come to campus. The Illinois county in which DuPage is located has a high growth rate, excellent high schools, and a well-educated population. One person interviewed at the school said that it "is hard to believe the College of DuPage could fail in anything it was doing given the immense force of the community."

An example of a small private college oriented toward its community is Queens. A national publication said, "The way Queens administrators talk about 'service,' one might imagine they wear the word emblazoned on sweatshirts." When Billy Wireman became president, he stated that no serious fund raising could occur before the needs of the community were assessed and met. He maintained, "You've got to be an investment, not a chartity."

One example of how Queens College has chosen to serve the community is Queens Compute, a personal computer training center established for personal and corporate needs. A faculty member associated with Queens Compute says, "We have the resources to make people and personal computers into effective human teams."

The University of Georgia, as a land-grant institution, is deeply concerned with its state-wide educational responsibilties. This concern is reflected in the university's "Nine Initiatives for the Nineties" program, as the school is driven by a determination to serve all the citizens of Georgia.

Schools like Carnegie-Mellon and Rensselaer, and the smaller private colleges, have a different definition of community from the schools mentioned previously. These institutions are linked to national communities, but are especially dependent on their immediate area for monetary support. In the cases of Carnegie-Mellon University and Rensselaer Polytechnic Institute, the community includes (1) the national engineering and scientific establishment; (2) an alumni group from all 50 states; and (3) the national research and development community. In addition, these schools are concerned with peer institutions, foundations, and the national media. However, relations with the surrounding geographical area are also of great importance. Both of these institutions are considered by their states to be valuable economic assets, and that revenue generating role is one of which these schools are very much aware, reflecting the importance of local relations to their own financial support.

Individual Initiative—Room for the Better Idea

We found an atmosphere allowing individuals throughout the institution to exercise initiative at all of our strategically oriented schools on the move. Examples of the encouragement of initiative and the results of such encouragement abound at these 20 schools. One such example is the recently unveiled cooperative fellowship program established between the University of Maryland-College Park and Fairchild Industries at the instigation of Lee Davidson, head of the electrical engineering department.

Such an initiative-generating atmosphere seems to be a function of two factors. The first is a universally understood institutional development plan, based on the strategic mission, which frees faculty to excercise individual initiative and at the same time help advance the institution as a whole. The second factor is administrators who create an atmosphere of freedom to apply skills and exercise creativity, but also allow for the consequeces of mistakes.

Aquinas, in support of its move toward age integration, has earmarked money for faculty incentive grants (FIGS) in an effort to encourage faculty to explore new options.

The willingness to accept certain risks and promote a risk-taking attitude is epitomized by George Low of Rensselaer, who stated, "Without risk, there can be no gain."

At the University of Tulsa there is a general feeling that individuals make a difference. One participant in administrative life said, "I get credit and recognition for what I do."

There is great latitude at Alverno for faculty to be creative. Alverno's encouragement of individuality provides a stimulating and challenging environment in which to work and study, according to several faculty and students interviewed. Indeed, there is an expectation that everyone will search for new ideas to enhance the mission of the college, a mission that is strongly oriented toward excellent teaching. While the work-load tends to be heavy for faculty and staff because of high expectations and the decision-making responsibilities placed on them, there is an almost unanimous feeling of personal satisfaction and a high level of commitment.

"Sometimes the faculty become frustrated because they cannot think of enough new things to try here," says DuPage's provost Ted Tilton, a statement succinctly expressing the school's encouragement of initiative. McAninch has created a $150,000 development fund to be used to encourage faculty, staff, administrators, and students to experiment and explore. Called the President's Risk Fund, this resource is available to anyone in the institution for the financing of any project that might enhance the life of DuPage.

Kennesaw College strongly encourages and supports individual initiative. Much of what has gone on at the college has occurred because of the work of particular individuals. The chair of the Department of Health, Physical Education, and Recreation, for example, recently proposed some new curricular ideas for her department, including combining physical education and outdoor recreation with computer technology, which will soon be implemented.

Harry Downs assumed the presidency of Clayton Jr. College somewhat discontented with what junior colleges were offering the public. He knew that general education could be improved, and he believed that colleges ought to be able to identify what it is that they expect students to learn. Downs, however, had no specific plan to effect such changes. Every year when he addressed the faculty, Downs talked about these issues, and a few minor curriculum reform efforts resulted. In 1979, a new faculty member, Linda Greer, heard the president's annual address and attempted to find a solution to this problem. As a result of her initiative, she became the catalyst for the outcome-focused, assessment-based general education program that is now Clayton's major thrust.

Commitment to the Institution—Loyalty and Allegiance

Perhaps the most important characteristic of an organizational saga is capturing allegiance, committing the staff to the institution. At all of the schools we examined, an effort to build commitment to the institution is an integral part of the overall college mission. Commitment is solidified by encouraging participation, ensuring opportunity for individual initiative, and building a sense of common purpose through a strategic mission. As individual and institutional initiatives become successful and goals are achieved, greater outside recognition is gained and faculty, students, and staff begin to take a renewed pride in the institution, which in turn reinforces commitment. This process, once underway, seems to be self-perpetuating.

A professor of psychology at Bradford College told of the despair she felt previously when she attended professional meeetings and only heard expressions of concern about conditions at her college. Now when she is present at these meetings she finds her spirits lifted as people want to know about the "exciting new Bradford." She and other faculty members say they return to campus from such gatherings with a renewed sense of purpose and a determination to keep the school on track toward its goals.

Norbert Hruby's first undertaking as president of Aquinas was the implementation of an extensive self-study. As part of this self-study, 28 teams composed of faculty, staff, and administrators visited 28 colleges that were doing something of interest to Aquinas. The curious result of the visitation venture was that those people who believed that Aquinas College, like Mary Poppins, was "practically perfect in every way," saw that it could be improved, and those who thought it was hopeless came to recognize that it had promise. Throughout the Hruby years, with the self-study and visitation efforts as a foundation, pride in Aquinas and commitment to it have grown.

Commitment to Marylhurst College was vividly demonstrated by the faculty two years ago when, during a temporary financial crisis, they voted to return 20% of their salaries to the school. This altruistic move illustrates the depth of commitment felt by this faculty, who were dedicated to the idea that their school would survive.

There is an immense pride throughout Alverno concerning the school's present agenda and its future plans. Commitment to quality teaching and an emphasis on students is not only fostered but is expected of faculty and staff. Finally, morale is high at Alverno in part because faculty are made to feel that their efforts are important contributions to the common cause.

Kennesaw College aspires to be a model four-year school for the state system of Georgia. Staff and students alike seem to be delighted to be a part of the school. A faculty member wrote, in a letter to one of our interviewers, "It was not only encouraging for us to know that there are others who realize the excellence here at Kennesaw, but I hope we have conveyed to you a sense of excitement, quality innovation, and team spirit which is the basis for us being a college on the move."

Concern for Students and Faculty—Campuses with Heart

Two distinct views regarding their constituencies were apparent among the institutions examined: There was an almost familial interest in the faculty and staff; and there was an intense concern for the quality of the education provided for students. These attitudes were reflected in the strategic mission statement at virtually every insitution included here.

An orientation toward faculty was exhibited in several ways among these schools, such as efforts to encourage staff to make investments in an institution and its future, and policies of retraining rather than laying off or firing employees during times of retrenchment.

At Northern Arizona University, classes are kept small and student advising is an important priority with faculty and administrators alike extensively involved in the campus advising center. Additionally, the college is dedicated to helping the local Native American population meet its needs by taking many of its special programs off campus onto reservations and by directing attention to the health care needs of the Navajo and Hopi tribes.

Northeast Missouri State exhibits its concern for students through, among other things, its value-added learning programs. President McClain hopes that the school's graduates will be able to compete on a national level of quality and excellence.

President Downs of Clayton Jr. College says the attitude that students are important is one of the driving forces at his college. Faculty members interviewed confirmed this sentiment, but Downs made the most telling comment when he said that his hope was that Clayton Jr. College would produce "joyful learners." Several senior faculty members confirmed that, above all else, Downs has always insisted that the interest and concerns of students be the top priority of the institution. A student interviewed said, "I'm not easy to please, but this school has the attitude that the student is a customer and is always right. That makes you want to give a little."

The School of Education at Kennesaw College claims "active student involvement" as an important component of its programs. Students in that school serve on advisory boards and are actively involved in the search process when faculty are recruited. "The students see the program as *their* program—one to which they contribute as well as go through. This may be the most important feature of our program," said one member of the faculty. KC 101, a class that consists of an academic orientation to Kennsaw, is an example of the school's desire to enhance the overall experience of entering students. An assistant professor of psychology writes: "I believe strongly in this course and have seen it put both spark into dormant minds and energy into lethargic bodies (the minds and bodies reference does not refer solely to the students!) Plus, it is fun to teach."

Bradford's plan for the liberal arts, Clayton's competency-based plan, and Northeast Missouri's value-added plan are all focused on giving the full-time undergraduate an unsurpassed liberal arts education.

At Rensselaer, research is considered an important teaching tool, and the inclusion of undergraduates in funded faculty research projects is considered a way to enhance their education. At Carnegie-Mellon, the use of computers in the education process greatly enhances the students' practical experience and the value of their college training, as computers become an ever more integral part of our culture's functioning.

Colleges such as DuPage, Queens, Aquinas, Marylhurst, and Maricopa have extended their concern for students' education to part-time adult learners. These schools are determined to see that nontraditional students receive a quality education, and have made major structural and programmatic efforts in that direction, beyond revising class schedules and advisement services, although these are important adjustments.

The Future is Now—Opportunity Consciousness

Peck (1983) found opportunity consciousness to be the second-most-important characteristic of the 20 small "successful" colleges he studied in 1981. We also found this to be a crucially important trait of our 20 institutions on the move. However, at the schools we examined, opportunity consciousness is a characteristic found not only among presidents, but also among boards and faculty.

One important piece of evidence showing the opportunity consciousness present in boards at these schools can be found by examining the presidential selection process at several of these institutions. The Bradford board of trustees, searching for someone with a clear vision of the future, hired Arthur Levine and his practical liberal arts plan. Rensselaer tapped George Low, who was not an academic but who did have strong ideas about the institution's future, as an alumnus and former board member.

Opportunity consciousness is manifest by an attention to the future. Maricopa Community College District is pursuing a $15 million grant from a computer company, for state of the art equipment. Personal computers will be available to all faculty and administrators. Rio Salado College, "The Campus Without Walls," is rapidly becoming nationally known. It addresses centrally the educational needs of nontraditional students who will become the most important cohort of the future.

Betty Siegel of Kennesaw defines intelligence as "the capacity to sense an opportunity and make it work for you." President Siegel says, in a Cobb County Publication in the fall of 1984,

> I think one of the most important things that could happen in this college would be to have a fine building that could be a performing arts center. Kennesaw College already handles the Cobb County Symphony and we're working with a proposal to have a dance company join us. We have all these beautiful artists in Cobb County and in the counties to the north of us, and they need a gallery worthy of their efforts.

Siegel obviously makes opportunites.

At Clayton Jr. College, Harry Downs' ability to sense opportunity is evident when he speaks about continuing education, which he considers the second major area of emphasis at Clayton. Business and industry are booming in the area around the compus, and Downs considers the potential for educational programming to be practically unlimited. In 1984 when the automotive industry began to become revitalized, the Hapeville Ford plant was selected to manufacture the Taurus, Ford's new high tech car designed to compete with imports. The plant began to recall workers, both local and national, many of whom had been out of work for years. Clayton Jr. College helped with the planning and then hosted an intensive six-week orientation for the returning workers who would constitute the second shift. Each of the 1300 returning workers underwent a 40-hour training program. When they returned to work, something unprecedented occurred—the second shift outperformed the first shift. The following summer, when the plant closed for six weeks to remodel for its new venture, Clayton hosted the Ford Summer Institute, a series of training programs for first-line supervisors with many different educational opportunities. These programs have led Clayton into a similar training venture with General Motors.

Virtually all of the strategic missions developed at schools mentioned here and the resulting initiatives address serious contemporary societal concerns regarding higher education. Quality undergraduate education, value-added and competency-based instruction, private support for building quality, high technology, and excellence in teacher education represent crucial areas of intersection for education's outcomes and society's needs and areas in which on-the-move schools are making their presence felt.

Quality—The Holy Grail

All of these schools on the move focus on excellence: both in their present programs, and, more importantly, in the future for which they are planning. In each of these schools there is evidence that the quality of the institution has improved significantly in recent years and is getting still better.

The typical institutional scenario among this group is as follows: First, a school focuses on a level of excellence that it hopes to achieve at some future date. Next, as the institution begins to enjoy some successes, and as the discussion of its future identity broadens and intensifies, the envisioned goal appears more and more attainable. Perceptions develop about the institution's rank in the academy, its quality, and its future, based on progress that is, in reality, short of the self-established goal of the school. However, perceptions become reality as prophecy becomes self-fulfilling.

An example of this pattern occurs at Northern Arizona with a declared strategy of "excellence, one college at a time." When forestry's position became secured, Northern Arizona President Hughes turned his attention to education, and in a bold move created the "Center of Excellence in Education" (see page 61).

With its Center of Excellence in Education a reality, the university has now turned its attention to the College of Business/School of Hotel and Restaurant Management. According to Hughes, "Those three programs provide us with a real thrust for the next decade and give us some distinctiveness."

George Mason University president George Johnson refers to the perception-reality strategy as the "smoke and mirrors" approach that he used to build a nationally recognized School of Information Technology and Engineering.

In 1980, without a graduate faculty in science and engineering, without even a department of engineering, and with only 13 engineers on the faculty, George Mason declared its intention to become a first-rate high technology school. Johnson formed an advisory board of high tech company chief executive officers, began a high technology seminar series, and established two undergraduate engineering programs. Considerable internal, regional, and state discussion followed. Industry leaders in the area committed themselves to five endowed professorships and $2 million in other assistance, and flexed their economic muscles at the state's political leaders. Soon after, the state of Virginia authorized six new master's programs and a doctoral program in computer engineering and computer science. As George Mason's reputation as an institution committed to high technology continued to expand, nationally recognized faculty began to migrate to the university and the state legislature put up $15 million to help advance the engineering programs. Perception continues to become reality at George Mason.

A perception-to-reality change is also demonstrable in the way an institution views its future. Continual focusing on the future—that is, on performance and quality levels above those of the present—appears to influence faculty behavior positively. Self-interest and institutional reinforcement cause movement toward that future ideal, through present action and the belief that goals are closer than they seem. This attitude changes internal procedures and attracts a higher caliber of faculty and students.

At Queens College concern about the future is evidenced in Queens '90, "an academic/financial blueprint for the remainder of this decade." This document outlines the type of institution Queens should be in 1990 and the financial resources necessary to effect the transformation.

Another example of Queens orientation toward the future is

Project Renaissance, a plan to build the College of Arts and Sciences into "one of the most future-oriented and distinctive undergraduate, church-related colleges for women in the country" by combining liberal arts and career preparation.

Summary

These diverse and interesting institutions, although in many ways different, do share many common qualites. They share something else: the motivational forces which set them on the path toward new levels of effectiveness, excellence, and recognition. Those three factors are their *locations*, which were either initially positive or negative; *adversity,* generally focused 10 years or more ago in the early 1970s; and *leadership,* which was the only one of the three present to a significant degree in each institution.

Chapter 3 explores those factors in depth with a great deal of attention being devoted to analysis of the leadership styles and common qualities of the presidents.

These 10 characteristics can be found individually at many schools other than the ones that were a part of our study. However, what makes these traits important is their aggregation at particular schools—these institutions, through a combination of factors (including luck), have developed these traits as fundamental parts of their character. We have provided what we believe is an X ray; we have outlined the skeleton around which these colleges and universities have fleshed out their program. Chapter 2 provides insight into the causes spurring the development of these traits, and into the process that enables a school to outshine its peers, particularly in leadership.

The Motivating Forces: Location, Adversity, and Leadership

It was an excellent location for a college—in 1824—and for over 100 years thereafter, Troy, New York, remained Edenic. Just up the Hudson River from the nation's premier commercial center, New York City, and at the eastern terminus of the young country's then-most innovative transportation system, the Erie Canal. Troy was at the heart of American industrialization in the first half of the nineteenth century.

Rensselaer Polytechnic Institute (RPI) was established in Troy in 1824 as the nation's first engineering school (if the military academy at West Point is not considered strictly an engineering school), and became the model for many other engineering schools founded across the country during the nineteenth century—Carnegie Tech, Case Tech, Rice Institute, Lehigh, and others—as the United States spread westward, becoming a world economic and industrial power.

Upstate New York kept pace with the nation's progress for over a century, but after World War II, forces building momentum since 1900 began to affect RPI environment; the school found that being at one end of the Erie Canal was not the advantage it once was. The golden era ended in 1959 with the opening of the St. Lawrence Seaway, which made all of the Great Lakes ports seaports and greatly diminished the importance of the New York canals.

The opening of the seaway coincided with another development that spelled trouble for RPI. Paradoxically, this was the launching of the Russian satellite Sputnick, which initiated a major national emphasis on science and engineering in the United States.

The resulting massive increases in federal and state aid for college and university science and engineering programs accelerated a process that had been underway since the 1940s—the building of major engineering education and research centers throughout the nation. New centers for the discipline rapidly developed at places such as the University of California at Berkeley, Stanford University, Colorado State, Texas A & M, the University of Texas at Austin, Arizona State, and others. While institutions like the Massachusetts Institue of Technology were able to take advantage of this national trend, others such as RPI found no comparative advantage in the situation. The school was not declining; rather, RPI simply did not keep up with the new kids on the block.

These competitors had taken their toll on RPI by the late 1960s. According to Keller (1983: p. 80), "The college (RPI), once a pioneer in engineering education, had fallen far behind by the 1960s. Academic leadership and fund raising were weak. Many of the buildings and laboratories had kept their pre-World War II charm and grime." Open rebellion against the college's administration began to be expressed among the faculty, including such moves as a vote on faculty unionization by the mid-1970s—actions unusual at a major private institution, especially for an engineering professoriate.

The Rensselaer story illustrates how crucially important location can become for many institutions of higher education. For most of its life RPI's location was a tremendously positive force, pushing the college forward in good times and bad. Then, after World War II, RPI's local environment became an increasingly negative factor in the institution's growth and development; however, these same detrimental effects made the college receptive to change and innovation —specifically, to new leadership.

Time and again in our study of colleges on-the-move we found institutions whose location created a climate conducive to a great leap forward. In some cases general location and/or regional demographics created an adverse environment that prepared a college community for major changes, and sparked a desire for new leadership. In others, the community was a positive influence, growing and developing so rapidly that the particular school was forced to change—and fast—just to keep up.

Strength Through Adversity

Adversity was a significant factor in the recent evolution of Carnegie-Mellon University, and Bradford, St. Norbert, Aquinas, Alverno, and Marylhust colleges. These schools found themselves in crisis sitations regarding their future, but each found the will and the crucial leadership to work its way to stabiltiy.

Carnegie-Mellon University was founded at the turn of the twentieth century with money from two steel fortunes in Pittsburgh, a booming steel town. The university was created to be a premier technological institute. After decades of growth and development Carnegie-Mellon found its position to be precarious in the early 1970s, the decline of the steel industry and its concomitant effects on Pittsburgh itself brought about five consecutive years of budget deficits for Carnegie-Mellon. The school was ready for change.

St. Norbert College in Green Bay, Wisconsin was dramatically affected by two forces in the mid-to-late1960s. First, the college's relative importance to the Green Bay community was permanently altered by the founding of the University of Wisconsin-Green Bay in 1968. Following this event came the general enrollment downturn of the early 1970s, which hit the frostbelt earlier than the rest of the country. The net result shook St. Norbert to its very foundations, but also paved the way for the radical changes necessary for the school's survival.

Sink or Swim!

Growing populations, strong economic development, and technological expansion have combined to create dynamic local environments that have forced institutions such as the universities of Maryland and Tulsa, George Mason University, and colleges such as Maricopa, DuPage, and Kennesaw to accelerate their development and growth just to keep from being overwhelmed.

Being located at both ends of the Washington-Baltimore corridor, in an explosively developing high tech commercial center, the University of Maryland has both wanted and been forced to compete nationally. The change in the university's surrounding community accelerated in the late 1960s and early 1970s, when the federal government began contracting out services, particularly applied research, to new high tech companies, and as high technology began to emerge as a critical component of the national defense establishment. The growth of local sophisticated companies attracted highly educated scientists, engineers, and managers to the area, professionals who had come from Route 128, Boston, and San Jose where educational institutions are nationally known for their excellence. Being viewed through the eyes of a new and elite business community made the University of Maryland uncomfortable with its traditional identity, and created the requisite environment for the installation of a new and dynamic leader.

Several other institutions in our study faced situations similar to that experienced by Maryland. The Maricopa colleges are located in Phoenix, the epitome of a growing Sunbelt city, while the College of DuPage is located in a large county—the home of the Argonne and Fermi laboratories and a highly educated citizenry—just outside Chicago. The University of Tulsa, Kennesaw College, and George Mason University are all located in dynamic communities that have great expectations for their educational institutions.

In only one case did we find a college located in an exceptionally dynamic community that had experienced genuine adversity. Charlotte, North Carolina, is the center of the fastest growing section of one of the most dynamic states in the South. Queens College is one of only three institutions of higher education in Charlotte. (A fourth, Davidson College, is located in a small town just outside Charlotte.) Founded in 1857 as a Presbyterian finishing school for young women, Queens and its companion school for young men at Davidson had the Charlotte area to themselves for several generations.

However, the 1960s brought many changes to the region. Two public institutions in Charlotte that had been quietly growing suddenly came into their own in that decade—Central Piedmont Community College and the University of North Carolina at Charlotte. These two schools became increasingly important to the economic development of the region during the 1970s, while Queens became relatively less important. In addition, the enrollment problems faced by many institutions as the decade unfolded hit Queens (and Davidson) hard.

Davidson responded to the demographic crunch by going coed. This made the situation at all-female Queens even more critical. Queens had many problems, including deficits, dropping enrollments, and an overbuilt physical plant financed by expected revenues from future enrollment increases. The school had banked a great deal of good will from the Charlotte community, but no one seemed to know how to capitalize on that asset. When the search for a new president began in 1977, the college community was focusing on the importance of strong leadership and was eminently ready for new ideas.

The forces that started each of these 20 schools on-the-move toward new levels of effectiveness and excellence were spawned in the 1960s and early 1970s. In the majority of instances, a crisis situation or the effects of a dynamic community caused an institution to seek strong and creative leadership, and a new direction. In the other cases a serendipitous combining occurred, between an institution simply looking toward its future and an individual with a vision searching for a place to make this a reality.

The one characteristic shared both by those schools in our sample exhibiting decisive change as a result of adversity and those merely keeping up with the times was the presence of a visionary and driving leader. How did these 20 institutions happen to get just the right match? Was it luck? In truth, exactly what kind of leaders did they get?

CHAPTER 3

Leadership: The Critical Element

Challenging Conventional Wisdom—Portrait of a Leader

For Gene Hughes, 1983 was a watershed year. Hughes, the president of Northern Arizona University, had been appointed to the Arizona State Board of Education by the state's governor shortly after taking the helm at NAU in 1979, and 1983 was the fourth year of his service. (In Arizona, one of the three university presidents serves on the state board of education.) Coincident with Hughes's term on the state board, a number of forces that had been building for more than a decade coalesced into a national fervor concerning the quality of public schools in America, a wave of concern that crested in 1983 when the U.S. Department of Education released the report of its Commission on Excellence, *A Nation at Risk.*

Like its counterparts across the country, the Arizona State Board of Education spent a lot of hours discussing reform in curriculum, financing, standards, teacher pay scales, teacher education (both preservice and in-service), and many other issues. As a board member, Gene Hughes found himself learning almost more than he wanted to know about the problems and challenges of America's secondary and elementary schools.

Because of his board position, Hughes attended two of a series of national conferences (at Colorado Springs, Colorado and New Haven, Connecticut) at which were present chief state school officers from all 50 states and one college president from each of the states. On these occasions he had the opportunity to talk with many of the top higher education thinkers, especially concerning such things as the preparation and training of teachers, counselors, and administrators.

In the course of these meetings and others, Hughes also was able to discuss some of the ideas and research that would later become Clark Kerr's *Presidents Make a Difference,* a study of the college presidency published in 1985, which concluded that today's presidents are virtual figureheads. Hughes, believing that the problems plaguing elementary and secondary schools are massive and pervasive, wondered, "Is there anything that an individual university president could do to begin to alleviate some of the widespread malaise? Can a president make a difference?"

While these thoughts occupied him, in November of 1983 Gene Hughes attended a meeting of the American Association of State Colleges and Universities and heard a speech by Paul Woodring concerning AASCU-type institutions and teacher training. Many AASCU member institutions had been established as normal schools, had then become state teachers colleges, and finally emerged as regional state universities—Woodring made the telling point that schools with teacher training as their original raison d'être, such as Northern Arizona, should be the ones to take the lead in responding to criticisms of America's educational system. This directive stuck in Gene Hughes's mind, taking root amid the ideas gleaned from his travels.

Upon his return to Flagstaff after the AASCU meeting, one of Hughes's first orders of business was finding a new chair to head the curriculum and instruction department in the College of Education. In addition, Northern Arizona would soon be seeking people to fill several leadership positions in its education college—the chairs of the educational psychology and educational administration departments, the associate dean of education, and possibly others.

When the number of these major education college positions to be filled dawned upon Hughes, he said to himself, "Why should all these positions be filled using a traditional model? Why not take this opportunity to do something different?" All the ideas he had absorbed in conferences and discussions began to come together in a new plan.

In a two-week period, Hughes and his staff put together a totally different approach to teacher education, an approach centered around something that they labeled "the Center of Excellence in

Education." (For a detailed description, see Part II.) Using this fresh formulation, they proposed to abolish the traditionally structured College of Education; with this move, Northern Arizona University would start down a new and uncertain path.

In a whirlwind 40 days, President Hughes went to the university's board of regents, the state board of education, the governor, and the Arizona legislature, and received the go-ahead for his Center of Excellence and a special $1 million appropriation. In Hughes's words, "We were off and running."

Few people on campus in Flagstaff knew of these dramatic moves until Hughes called a general faculty meeting and announced them as follows: The College of Education was abolished, and its dean was off to another university to assume a similar post. Taking the place of the old college was the new Center of Excellence in Education, with a state-wide mission and a unique administrative structure topped by a vice president instead of a dean. A bold move was made, and while only the future can provide an answer concerning the wisdom of Northern Arizona's creation, the first annual report of the Center of Excellence in Education is upbeat and full of promise, documenting the center's success so far. Gene Hughes can take a bow.

TWO MYTHS

What really happened at Northern Arizona was that two tenets of current thinking in academe were shown to be convention, not wisdom. One of these is the belief that colleges and universities can and do nothing major to improve teacher education. Concerning the second, the actions of Gene Hughes provided an effective counter argument to the idea, given strong voice by Clark Kerr, that strong leadership is virtually impossible in contemporary America, and especially in colleges and universities.

How the Northern Arizona Center for Excellence in Education turns out is another story. What is important here is that Gene Hughes was insightful enough to see an opportunity to take an entirely different approach to an acknowledged national problem —and he was able to act. Northern Arizona's experiment in teacher education is radically new. It is the first such effort in the nation to get a state-wide mandate analogous to the agricultural teaching, research, and extension programs of the land-grant colleges. The center is headed by a university vice president instead of a dean because it is now central rather than peripheral to the university's mission. Its stucture was quite different from other education programs and schools, and was innovative and reponsive enough to attract support and resources from the state's public and private leadership. Finally, the center shares a position of state priority equivalent to Arizona State Uuniversity's Center for Excellence in Engineering.

The story of Northern Arizona University and its president, Gene Hughes, is but one example of an institution moving boldly to secure a place in the sun. Other schools and their own stories, and those of the men and women who lead them, are what is reported in this book. We believe something exciting is happening at the grass-roots level in American higher education. The sounds being heard on America's campuses are those of conventional wisdom being shattered—leadership *can* be exercised, goals *can* be accomplished, and higher education *can* be master of its fate.

The Leadership Question

We began our study with the assumption that leadership would be a crucially important factor in initiating institutional advancement and, even more importantly, in providing the drive fueling such movement. This assumption was proven correct; indeed, it clearly was far more crucial than we had speculated.

When we started our research it seemed appropriate just to go out and observe what was going on at the 20 institutions, but it was also necessary to have a frame of reference providing for cross-institutional consistency. The question of how to develop a frame of reference for analyzing the characteristics of leadership led us to the literature concerning leadership, where we searched for leadership styles that might be appropriate to institutions of higher learning.

In Search of Excellence showed us one style. In their book, Peters and Waterman discussed Leavitt's description of the management process as an interaction of three variables—path finding, decision making, and implementing. They concluded that leadership could also be characterized by these variables and that any one leader would possess a combination of the three, but with only one dominant variable.

Basically defined, path finders give direction and are visionary; decision makers are preoccupied with details; and implementers pull people together to get things done. As examples, the authors classified John F. Kennedy as a path finder, Robert McNamara and Jimmy Carter as decision makers, and Lyndon Johnson as an implementer.

Drucker (1970) defined management as being composed of three functions—entrepreneurship, administration, and public relations. Cohen and March (1974) were able to characterize college presidents in terms of three roles—entrepreneur, administrator, and political leader—by analyzing time-utilization patterns. According to their findings the average small college president functioned more as a entrepreneur, while the president at a medium-sized institution was mostly an administrator; at large institutions, the leader spent more time involved with political activities.

Aside from the structure of their professional roles, we were also interested in these 20 leaders as people. Are they hard-driving (everyone get out of the way or get run over) or are they compassionate? Are they open to ideas and criticism? Are they visible on campus? What kind of public relations skills do they possess?

Using these questions and the results of a literature survey, we developed a leadership questionnaire (Appendix B). The four general queries listed previously were presented to over 200 people interviewed during campus visits, excluding the 20 presidents. The president's ratings on the 18 descriptors (Appendix B) were also gathered from all those involved except presidents.

To help complete the picture, the following open-ended questions were specifically directed to the presidents in this study: What is your reaction to Clark Kerr's study of the presidency? How do you feel about your working environment? What has been your greatest obstacle to getting things done at your institution?

The responses to our questions, obtained through interviews during field visits, and other information such as newspaper articles, biographies, and speeches, allowed us to delineate many qualities shared by our 20 presidents. These characteristics are itemized in subsequent sections of this chapter. First, however, we needed to know more about these men and women as individuals—where did they come from? Are they different from the general population of college presidents. Who are they?

Biographical Profile of 20 Presidents

In the process of studying these successful institutions and their leaders, we collected extensive biographical data on the men and women at the top level of administration, the presidents and chancellors. From these data we have isolated some characteristics that distinguish these people from college and university leaders in general. Specifically, this special group differed in three areas from their counterparts: age and tenure in office, academic preparation, and previous experience (specifically their position just prior to assuming their latest office).

The average age of the 20 presidents and chancellors in 1985 was 55 years, with a range between 36 and 66 years. This group's average tenure in office as of 1985 was 10.3 years, with the tenure range between 3 and 18 years.

These figures indicate that these men and women were, on the average, 45 years old when they assumed their current office. Kerr (1985) reported that, nationally, presidents enjoy an average tenure of seven years, which is two-thirds the average tenure of the 20 presidents and chancellors we studied.

Of the group in our study, 18 have an earned doctorate—and the other two have worked beyond the master's degree but do not hold a Ph.D. Considered by disciplinary areas, the group is composed as follows: nine received their highest degree in education, followed by two in English, and one each in sociology, history, psychology, economics, law, physics, mathematics, veterinary medicine, and engineering. Each of the five community college presidents' highest degree is in education, and two of the four AASCU-class institution heads also did their academic work in education.

Table 3.1 shows the positions of the 20 presidents before their

TABLE 3.1
The Presidents' Previous Positions

	20 ON-THE-MOVE INSTITUTIONS	CHRONICLE 1983-84	CHRONICLE 1973-74
President	6 (30%)	24 (22%)	27 (23%)
Vice President	7 (35%)	58 (53%)	49 (41%)
Dean	2 (10%)	16 (15%)	10 (8%)
Professor	3 (15%)	3 (3%)	19 (16%)
Other Academic/ Federal/State Government	3 (10%)	8 (7%)	14 (12%)
Total	21 (100%)	109 (100%)	119 (100%)

present jobs. For comparative purposes we reviewed all new appointment announcements in the *Chronicle of Higher Education* for the academic years 1973-74 and 1983-84. The results of this review are presented in the following table.

These data indicate several trends when the two years are compared, along with some differences among the 20 institutional leaders. The national figures indicate that the percentage of newly appointed presidents who came from another presidency was relatively stable, being 23% in 1973-1974 and 22% 10 years later. Between 1973-74 and 1983-84 the percentage of new presidents coming from a vice presidency jumped from 41 to 53; however, during this decade there has been a substantial drop-off in the percentage of professors/chairs being appointed to a presidency.

In comparing the presidents of our colleges on-the-move with the 106 presidents whose appointments were reported in the *Chronicle of Higher Education* in 1983 and 1984, we found some striking differences. In general, our 20 presidents and chancellors were more likely to come to their current position from other presidencies, other academic organizations and government, or from the ranks of professors/chairs. A significantly lower percentage of our group came from vice president, provost, or dean positions, compared to the *Chronicle of Higher Education* samples.

The Presidential Character

A majority of those at the helm of on-the-move institutions in this study share, according to our accumulated data, 10 common qualities that we have divided into two groups. The first group was determined by a consensus of the research team based on field studies and observation. According to these findings, the five characteristics in the first group are the following: (1) goal oriented; (2) intelligent; (3) persistent and hard working; (4) good at shaping their work environment; (5) compassionate.

The second group of characteristics was determined after we asked our 200 interviewees to evaluate their institution's president or chancellor on a number of items using a scale of 1 to 5, with 1 being "strongly disagree" and 5 being "strongly agree."

The accumulated data indicate the presidents as a group were rated at or above 4.5 on the following five presidential descriptions listed on the rating scale: (6) visionary; (7) opportunity conscious; (8) team builder; (9) good at public relations; (10) open.

The responses we received on these questionnaires were reinforced by field observations during our campus visits.

Using the numerical evaluations gathered during our field interviews we were also able to highlight four common characteristics of these campus leaders that contradicted the expectations we had concerning their character before we began our study. Generally speaking, these administrators were not controversial, did not work by the book, were not authoritarian, were not isolated on campus, and in most cases were not risk takers.

Presidential Qualities

In all, we have outlined 14 traits among this group. The following paragraphs describe the characteristics of these presidents in more detail.

INTELLIGENCE AND CREATIVITY

On campus after campus, one of the first comments we heard in interviews was "Our president is unusually intelligent." What is defined by "intelligent" takes varied forms at different campuses. In some cases, the president or chancellor was a serious scholar. Richard M. Cyert, president of Carnegie-Mellon, is an economist whose dissertation adviser was Arthur Burns, and who was a colleague of Nobel laureate Herbert Simon doing seminal work in industrial organization before assuming the presidency of Carnegie-Mellon University.

Other leaders we interviewed were accomplished scientists. John Slaughter, chancellor of the College Park campus of the University of Maryland, served as director of the National Science Foundation before taking his present position, and he has done distinguished work in electrical engineering.

When we asked faculty, staff, and administrators if their president was an "ideas person," they would immediately light up and respond vigorously. These leaders seem to be constantly on the lookout for ideas that could have practical value for their school.

FAR-RANGING VISION

Indeed, the key to this aspect of the presidential character as we have analyzed it was not the number of original ideas these leaders produced; rather, it was the fact that they seemed to have their antennae extended constantly, looking for ways to build and to strengthen their institution. A perceptive awareness of campus needs, coupled with an ability to assess an idea and bring possibility and reality together, was demonstrably present in almost every one of these men and women.

Chancellor Paul Elsner of the Maricopa Community College District "plants seeds—thousands of ideas," according to an interviewee. The president of one of the colleges in the district said, "He drives us crazy with his new ideas."

Neil Webb's ability to assess the potential of St. Norbert was evident, and badly needed, when he arrived. His innovative ideas, from campus beautification plans to the school's taking over food service functions, have been vital to the college's resurgence.

PERSISTENCE

As a corollary to the generation of ideas, one of the most important traits of this group is a sometimes dogged persistence—combined with the flexibility to adjust to changes as necessary. This combination is unusual, and of inestimable value in administration and the implementation of innovative changes.

Charles McClain of Northeast Missouri developed a value-added program over 12 years ago. However, he phased it in gradually—one step at a time over a 10 year period. McClain calls this the "I see the light" tactic. Testing of competency was at first voluntary—then required. Today, the program continues to evolve; the next step will be the required demonstration of competency before awarding a degree.

SHAPING THE WORKING ENVIRONMENT

A key element in the success of these leaders appeared to be the ability to shape and control their working environment. Billy Wireman told us, "You've got to run the job or it will run you." These men and women, by being proactive, establishing a good relationship with their boards, and consciously celebrating campus achievements and praising others along the way, create and shape their environment both physically and psychologically, which allows them to be even more effective.

Alverno College's Joel Read works well with her board, and her careful selection of faculty willing to commit themselves to the college's plans for advancement shows her attention to creating the environment she thinks most productive.

Richard Cyert is particularly adept at controlling his own working environment. He continually tries to shape his working situation by being proactive, forcing himself and his associates to think ahead, and always being involved in new initiatives. By doing so, others—internally and externally—react to his plans, conforming to his expectations.

At Maricopa, Paul Elsner controls his destiny by leading the board of trustees. One of the presidents in the Maricopa system said, "Elsner is a genius with the board. He exposes the board to a lot and keeps them informed. While he knows when to push, he also knows when to back off."

OPPORTUNITY CONSCIOUSNESS

Peck, in his 1983 study, defined opportunity consciousness as a leadership attitude whereby opportunities are expected to occur, opportunities to get things done, to advance the institution and help realize its potential despite all appearances to the contrary. Such opportunity consciousness is a continuing attention to changes in the environment, in the attitudes of people, and even in the values of society, to any change that can be turned to the advantage of the institution (1983: p. 5).

We would add to this definition the observation that the opportunity conscious president has a general concept of how his or her institution must change to be able to respond to inevitable environmental evolution. Such a president will try to position his or her institution to take advantage of future opportunities, without knowing specifically what these opportunities will be

Robert Smith, vice president for development at the University of Maryland, told us that John Toll had more insight into future events that would have an impact on universities like Maryland than anyone he had ever met. However, he said Toll had difficulty communicating this on campus because he could not relate specifics; He knew only the general direction the school must go and general future conditions, and tried to organize the university to take advantage of opportunities he knew would be coming in the years ahead.

Northern Arizona University president Gene Hughes was perceptive regarding both national and local needs in the field of education. He saw a unique opportunity, a chance to create a program not duplicated at sister institutions. Hughes abolished the School of Education at Northern Arizona and established a Center for Excellence in Education. Hughes's tactics were perfect: After seeing his chance, he put together a proposal in one week. At the end of six weeks he had won legislative approval for his plan and a $1 million appropriation. (To accomplish these feats of legerdemain the president bypassed the faculty.)

BUILDING AND SUSTAINING A TEAM

We found that most of these leaders realized the importance of building an administrative team and devoted much of the early period of their tenure to team building. In some cases this is done primarily by reshuffling, and in other cases there is wholesale replacement of personnel. In both cases team functioning is seen as a necessary component in the development of an institutional identity and a plan for the future.

The presidents profiled here, on the average, required between 12 and 18 months to get their leadership teams into place. As for the two types of team building we observed, an executive team constructed largely through internal promotions and reassignments seemed to begin functioning effectively sooner than one created largely through external appointments.

At Northern Arizona, many new people were brought into the ranks of the vice presidents and deans. (The average tenure of deans is three years.) Eugene Hughes believes in finding quality people and then giving them the freedom to act. One dean said, "I have more authority to act than anyone I know." There is an executive council, with evidence of considerable cooperation among its members.

At the University of Tulsa president Paschal Twyman states, "I find the strongest available talent, and then I'm permissive to the point of neglect." John Toll said at Maryland he wants "intellegent and compulsive people, the very best I can find."

Paul Elsner has built a top quality management team at Maricopa. According to those on campus, "He understands colleges need collegiality": he and his vice presidents work very closely. The Maricopa faculty are included in every aspect of campus activity, from the President's Council all the way down the organizational hierarchy.

FOSTERING GOOD PUBLIC RELATIONS

Good public relations are obviously enjoyed by all of these institutions: Each is nationally known, at least within the circle of its peer institutions. We found without exception that the schools in our study have excellent visibility in their local and state communities. Institutional initiatives and high profile activities account for the increased recognition they are enjoying. One of the major reasons for this recognition, however, we found as we visited campuses was that, even though approaches differ, all of these presidents have a knack for public relations.

Betty Siegel of Kennesaw College is particularly adept at public relations. Some of those on campus noted that the hopes of Kennesaw are founded on a strong liaison with the community. Siegel identified the necessity of this symbiosis early in her tenure, and she makes public relations a major focus of her presidential functioning.

Charles McClain is a master politician. He knows what will grab legislators' attention and produce dollars for his school. McClain is an articulate lobbyist: He is attempting to establish his institution as Missouri's liberal arts college; he is fighting the state's decision to discontinue programs in agriculture; he is a leading opponent of enrollment-driven funding formulas; and he has been instrumental in getting a $600 million state bond issue passed.

Paschal Twyman is a talented fund raiser with special strengths in the Tulsa community. He is involved in service groups and a statewide study group on high technology.

KEEPING THE DOOR OPEN

Finally, our analysis indicated that most of the presidents of these institutions on-the-move function openly and are accessible, communicating regularly with faculty and staff and the external community. They receive a great amount of input and are constantly scouting the campus and the community for information.

What is most important, these leaders have time for individual faculty and students. They are willing to listen, to have their ideas challenged, and even to be proven wrong. This did not mean that they frequently changed their minds when challenged; but, by being open and willing to listen and discuss, they have been able to minimize the resistance that normally builds up during the tenure of a president.

Harold MacAninch at DuPage meets on a monthly basis with student body representatives, faculty, and staff in a roundtable format.

Paul Elsner's staff feel they can "go to him with anything" or "stop him in the hall."

Charles McClain has an open-door policy. Even the students interviewed on campus saw him as open, receptive, and approachable.

The Mythical President

At the beginning of our study we compiled a list of characteristics that we felt would be part of the makeup of leaders driving institutions forward. We envisioned such persons as being controversial, highly organized by-the-book managers who were not very visible on campus, and were high risk takers and with authoritarian personalities. After we began our study, what we found was in fact the opposite of our composite president.

THROW THE BOOK OUT THE WINDOW

The presidents of these colleges on-the-move are considered effective at delegating, but they frequently cut across organizational lines to deliver a message, get some facts, or just see things for themselves. As a group, they are not overly concerned with organization and organizational matters; these leaders' concept of organizing is analogous to orchestra conducting.

Paul Elsner is not a fan of reports or accountability. One Maricopa director remarked, "All he asks for (formally) are my objectives once a year."

Paschal Twyman of Tulsa said, "I'm not big on organizational charts. I update mine once a year and then throw it in a drawer. People count." Generally, the presidents in our study liked to communicate directly with faculty face to face. In fact we were told that Cyert encouraged faculty to come to him with innovative proposals but that he handled it in a manner that would not disrupt the university.

A VISIBLE PRESENCE

We found these presidents to be, for the most part, visible on campus. For example, Art Levine, when on campus at Bradford, roams around freely from building to building and is seen by many people.

Eugene Hughes spends a lot of time at what he calls "hand shakers," meeting people and letting himself be seen in the college community. He spends a lot of time with students, often going to a residence hall for lunch.

CONSERVATIVE GAMBLERS

While several of the on-the-move presidents' institutions had indeed taken great risks as part of their institutional game plans, the majority of these leaders are not gamblers. Several did take great risk, such as Charles McClain, who in 1980 told the Missouri legislature he would raise the test scores of his students a certain percentage in exchange for an increased appropriation for the school. The legislators gave him the money, and he was able to uphold his end of this risky bargain. Perceiving the majority of these people as institutional risk takers, however, would be incorrect: While as far-seeing administrators they do articulate ambitious goals, these men and women work feverishly to minimize risk at every step of the way. One reason campus leaders may call themselves risk takers, and encourage this perception of themselves among others, is because as a group they urge people to be unafraid of failure.

NO LITTLE NAPOLEONS

Another conclusion of our field observations is that leadership style may vary, depending on the occasion and what is needed to ensure effective functioning. A president may be egalitarian one day, and authoritarian the next. While for the most part our presidents and chancellors were not the authoritarian figures we had posited, some variance did occur. The key to the matter seems to be, for a leader, building a base of support early—gaining respect and acceptance by being low key, pleasant, and noncontroversial. Once a solid base of trust has been established, presidents may occasionally take off on tangents in a unilateral and authoritarian manner. Because of the safety zone of good will they have created, however, constituents will usually tolerate this behavior.

COMPASSION—THE UNEXPECTED TRAIT

Most of the presidents at these schools were considered by those on campus to be compassionate to a degree we did not expect. When we asked those on campuses about the compassion of their president, an unusual number of persons gave concrete examples.

Harold McAninch has established a policy at DuPage providing that anyone displaced by a program's termination will be given the opportunity to retrain at the school's expense—with the expressed hope that the person will stay on at DuPage.

Paul Elsner has a strong personal touch: "He knows my family" was a common statement at Maricopa. In the fall of 1984 he rented a downtown Phoenix theater for an all-employee meeting, and spent two hours telling his staff and faculty what a good job they had done. Elsner also strongly supports "Project Vision," a program that attempts to help companies in the Maricopa district retrain rather than lay-off employees.

The Parallel Perspective

In 1978, Billy Wireman was sitting in his office at Rollins College in Florida, where he was head of the business program, when he received a telephone call from William Lee, chairman of Duke Power Company and head of a presidential search committee for Queens College. Lee said, "Dr. Wireman, we're looking for the right person to be president of Queens and we'd like to come down to Florida to talk to you."

Between that conversation and the committee's visit, Wireman had some time to think. He was comfortable with his situation at Rollins. Not only did he have a rewarding position at the college, but he and his family were running a successful restaurant on the booming east coast of Florida. However, Wireman knew well the reasons for the committee's interest, and his own interest was piqued.

Eleven years earlier, Wireman had taken over the presidency of deficit-ridden Florida Presbyterian College and within five years he had balanced the books, increased enrollment, developed a new strategic mission, and secured a $15 million endowment and a new name for the school—Eckerd College, in honor of the endowee (founder of a drugstore chain). After 10 years as president of Eckerd, Wireman felt he had finished the task he had originally set for himself and left to pursue other interests.

Wireman was aware of the problems at Queens and their similarity to those of Florida Presbyterian, and he knew that the resuscitation job he had performed at Eckerd was what had led the Queens committee to him. Queens College was ready for strong leadership and Wireman was ideally suited to provide such leadership. In fact, he took the job. What has enabled Wireman to perform his feats at Eckerd and Queens, and what led the shrewd Queens search committee to seek Wireman, was the bold and innovative plan that he brought to each school—an example of parallel perspective.

Perhaps the most telling quality we found among the leaders of our chosen institutions was something that we have labeled a "parallel perspective." These people came to their present jobs with a conceptual foundation on which they wished to build a plan for making major changes and for moving their school forward; usually a dramatic, wide-ranging, and detailed strategy with both general and specific applicability.

A corollary to the existence of this perspective is the observation that the institutions themselves, or at least those persons involved in selecting a president, had also decided that dramatic movement was crucial to their future: A quantum leap forward was needed and those involved in the search process knew incremental changes would not be adequate to ensure institutional health.

To compare our theory of parallel perspective to the reality of presidential searches in general around the country, we reviewed the process and the candidate chosen in 20 other searches that have taken place over the last two years. Search committee chairpersons, recently appointed presidents, and consultants involved in the search process indicated no sense of urgency about finding a place in the sun at any of these institutions. In fact, all involved seemed reluctant to admit to any anxieties about the future at all, or even to indicate the possibility that their institution had any needs aside from those that could be met by modest incremental changes in specific areas such as private fund raising. We sensed no desire on the part of these colleges for a president who would tamper with the educational program; if anything, in most of the cases there was usually resistance within the institution to choose such a person.

The elements of parallel perspective, as we found them among the presidents of the institutions in this study, were the following: (1) these presidents had spent a substantial amount of time before assuming the presidency studying a particular problem from a position combining detachment with a close-up view; (2) each had developed an approach to the problem in question that presented a unique opportunity for both the individual and the institution; (3) the schools that selected these persons to lead them had admitted their problems and put effort into solving them but had been unable to formulate a successful plan of attack on their own.

We have divided these different aspects into three categories delineating areas to which parallel perspective has been applied by various institutions in this study. These categories are: perspective concerning a problem, perspective concerning a type of institution, and perspective concerning a specific situation.

PERSPECTIVE ON A PROBLEM

We found several examples of presidents who were concerned with solving a specific problem in contemporary America or in higher education, and who, as heads of institutions, were given the opportunity to test their ideas.

Harry Downs served for some time as assistant chancellor of the Georgia higher education system, with special responsibility for two-year community colleges in the state. As he worked with these institutions, he began to perceive that they were not living up to their missions as teaching and learning institutions. By the time the Clayton Jr. College presidency became available, Downs had formulated specific ideas about how to focus on the instructional requirements of two-year open-door college students. Downs' ideas eventually provided the foundation for Clayton's "outcome-focused assessment-based education." This program has given Clayton Jr. College new life and made it distinctive in the Georgia system.

Neil Webb had a clearly defined plan for St. Norbert College when he assumed the presidency. He envisioned a total educational package built around the concept of group goals directed toward achieving quality in educational outcomes. Webb remembers well the vacation he took just before accepting the offer to become president of St. Norbert when he walked along a beach making notes in a black book (and drinking Maalox). Webb came back ready to tackle a tough job with a strategic plan in hand. Obviously, his perspective on this institution and its problems was a key factor in Webb's running start and successful performance.

Charles McClain of Northeast Missouri State University was ahead of his time. He felt that a college enrollment downturn was inevitable, and he began over 10 years ago to reorient his school toward an emphasis on quality. McClain characterized the mission of the university early in his administration: Programs would be broadened, standards for admission would be enhanced, and quality would be universally wide focus. McClain wanted to move his institution from its place as a teachers college to a new role as a small selective university. Obviously, McClain was ahead of his time in jumping on the quality bandwagon.

PERSPECTIVE ON AN INSTITUTION

During Harold McAninch's tenure as president at two small community colleges, he thought frequently about what could be done to convert a large community college into a national leader in its field. Taking over the presidency of the College of DuPage, a large suburban community college, McAninch implemented a deliberate approach to both administration and to relations with the external community that has resulted in DuPage's successful movement toward national prominence.

Kennesaw College, continues to change from a two-year institution into a comprehensive regional college with selected graduate programs. It is located in Georgia's fastest growing county, Cobb, which is challenging this young institution to keep up. Thus, Kennesaw required, at the time of Betty Siegel's arrival, extensive external development as well as attention to internal work. Siegel was experienced in both areas: Prior to coming to Kennesaw, she had served as academic dean for continuing education at the University of Florida, where she devoted most of her time to external relations. This was good training for the presidency of a new, growing college needing to get involved with a rapidly growing community.

Betty Siegel had also served as dean of the college of education at Western Carolina University where internal administration and curriculum development were institutional priorities—also good training for the head of a young, fast-developing college.

Each of these leaders had been concerned with the potential offered by a particular type of institution and each president made the most of an opportunity to implement their plans.

PERSPECTIVE ON A SITUATION

George Low was well versed in science and technology, and as an alumnus and board member of Rensselaer Polytechnic Institute he knew the school intimately.

Low also knew how to create a program with lofty goals—thanks to his years as deputy director of NASA. As he sat for several years of crisis on the RPI board of trustees, Low had the opportunity to develop a plan based on the university's environmental situation using science, industry connections, and government support to revitalize the school. Present president Berg told us the entire RPI community worked feverishly under Low's leadership for eight years to bring to fruition the president's "Rensselaer 2000" plan.

Another example of the parallel perspective occurred at Carnegie-Mellon University. For some 20 years prior to assuming the presidency of CMU, Richard M. Cyert, a student of organization, did two things concurrently. First, he shaped his ideas about how to develop and lead an effective organization through his research, teaching, and practicing of theory as a department head and then as dean of the Graduate School of Industrial Administration. Second, he kept one eye on the management and leadership of the total institution, observing it with the detached, but personally interested, eye of a true academic.

In developing his theories and trying them out, Cyert made the Carnegie-Mellon Graduate School of Industrial Administration a national leader. Instead of following Harvard, Wharton, and Sloan, he had those larger and wealthier institutions reacting to his school. Cyert may well have introduced the entire American higher education community to the concepts of strategic planning, comparative advantage, and distinctive niches by doing a few things well.

Cyert confirmed to us that he had a conceptual framework well developed upon entering the presidency. In fact, these ideas led him to immediately recall and produce a memorandum that he sent out on May 22, 1972, well over a month before he officially took over as president. Listen to Cyert in 1972:

> It has been clear to me for some time that this University needs an explicit statement of goals as well as a strategy for achieving them.

He asked several key questions which are today bouncing off the halls of academe with growing frequency. For example:

> In what specific areas in the field represented by the department does Carnegie-Mellon have a comparative advantage?
> Are there 'stars' in the fields that it would be critical to get into the department if we were to move?

It is clear to us that Richard Cyert has, through his thinking and practice and the communication of this work to the academy by George Keller and others, made a signal contribution to higher education in America. Without question, he brought a unique leadership perspective to Carnegie-Mellon and to American higher education.

The Successful Search

While these presidents themselves present instructive examples for institutions, perhaps the more important questions concern how the 20 colleges and universities chose their new leaders. How did these institutions recruit, select, and secure just the right individuals to be their presidents? Was it luck? Or did they do something right, something that can be transferred to other institutions?

These questions seemed important enough to explore, in depth, at five institutions where the match between institutions and individuals seemed exceptionally good and where the search process was recent enough to allow the compilation of detailed information. To examine these cases we conducted a series of interviews with key search committee members involved in the searches that resulted in the following matches: Harold McAninch at College of DuPage; George Johnson at George Mason; Billy Wireman at Queens; Arthur Levine at Bradford; and George Low at RPI.

On reviewing these five searches, we found four factors present among the institutions themselves that seemed to influence the final outcomes decisively. They are: a general consensus concerning each institution's situation, arrived at prior to the search (even designating the most important tasks facing the next president), the use of outside experts in a variety of formats; a dominant role by the governing board; and, an acceptance that the president's personal leadership style will likely dominate the institution to a significant degree.

THE CONSENSUS

In all five of these cases, the institution was less than happy with its situation. In several instances, deficits were undermining an institution's resources and posed a significant long-term threat to its viability. At DuPage and George Mason, the local community's expectations for the college far outpaced its capabilities and this gap was widening. In other cases, a proud, older institution could simply see itself slipping in relation to its peers and in relation to its own past performance. At all the schools, institutional problems were commonly understood by all constituency groups, there was no attempt to hide anything, and everybody involved knew that a unique and innovative leader was required.

THE SEARCH PROCESS

One college relied so heavily on a general purpose executive search firm that all the initial screening was completed by the outsiders, and the committee itself only saw seven applicants; in contrast, another college used a higher education executive search firm that gave all constituency groups a meaningful role in the process. At another school the search committee initially screened out half the nominees and applicants, then relied on two consultants to pare the remaining 100 candidates down to 7 semifinalists—at which time the committee again took charge. In still another case, consultants were used to check seven semifinalists. In each case, however, an outside consultant played a significant role.

THE GOVERNING BOARD

While in every case all constituency groups (faculty, students, alumni, etc.) were involved in some capacity, in some cases extensively—the governing board always made the final decision. This final decision was largely a function of candidate-board chemistry: in short, a subjective, unquantifiable decision.

THE IMPORTANCE OF THE PRESIDENT

It was clear in each of these searches that the personality of the candidate selected would tend to dominate the institution's "personality." Each committee seemed to be looking for a person whose public image would be virtually indistinguishable from that of the school, at least at some point in the future. Not that the committee's desire was for the basic character of the institution to be changed; most groups wanted to protect traditional values—rather, a new vision was desired, one that would build on traditional values.

Based on our conversations with members of these five search committees, we were able to formulate a set of rules that seem to have worked well in these instances. These rules are:

1. Establish a board-approved charter at the beginning of the search process, and be sure that all constituency groups are informed about its contents. Then, stick to the charter, even if one of the constituency groups decides that it wants to change things during the proceedings.
2. Make clear from the beginning that the governing board will make the final decision. This will help avoid confusion at a later critical point in the search.
3. Using an outside consultant with experience in search methodology and practices can be very helpful. The exact role of

such an outside entity is a function of the size and type of institution, its internal capabilities, and the time available for the search process.

4. Connect the search process in some way with the various constituency groups. There should be a feeling of community about the process—a feeling that everyone has been consulted and no one has been ignored. Again, the individual situation, institutional tradition, and search time-frame should influence the roles campus constituent groups play in the process.

5. Move as quickly as possible. While a board may very well decide to scrap a search and start over, when a pool of candidates is actually under consideration, time is of the essence.

6. Do not settle for a poor compromise—there should be a feeling on the board that the right person has been chosen to be president. While second choices, preselected candidates, and nice people may very well be able to do the job, the board should come out of the process feeling that it did a good job and that their choice is truly the best person for the job.

7. Maintain confidentiality. This is critical for it is not uncommon for a good person to withdraw when his candidacy becomes known prematurely at his/her current institution.

8. Observe carefully how a candidate presents himself or herself during the final round of interviews. This is a key factor in the selection process. Not only is a candidate's track record critical, but the candidate should also be able to present a clear statement of what his or her experience will mean to the new institution—style, skills, and vision are all important.

Our interviews revealed some additional insights that should be of interest to the higher education community. For example, in these five cases, securing a scholar to be president was not considered a priority—not even at RPI. In fact, academics seemed to be a secondary consideration, although it was clearly understood that an acceptable academic record was necessary.

Instead, leadership, defined as the ability to manage an organization, was the most important consideration. Commitment to sound financial management, and the aptitude, energy, and vision needed to set a direction and move an institution, were deemed to be critical.

It is difficult to quarrel with success. These five institutions have all enjoyed remarkable success with the presidents they chose. This summary of their approaches to the selection process, coupled with skill and concern, can provide useful insights for boards and help those seeking presidents to drive their school toward on-the-move status.

ATTRACTING EXCELLENT PRESIDENTS

One final question comes to mind: How do presidents view the selection process? What convinced these leaders to take on their new positions? To get the presidential perspective, we interviewed six presidents in our study and learned some interesting things.

First, the presidents who took these jobs saw each situation as a real challenge—the opportunity of a lifetime, according to several. They were not looking for a good-paying position presiding over a complacent institution that wanted someone to maintain the status quo. Further, it was readily apparent to all concerned from the very beginning that the institutions in question presented a real challenge. In fact, George Johnson told us that his initial contact with the search committee, in the form of a letter, clearly presented the George Mason job as an opportunity to really accomplish something. These men and women were clearly attracted and excited by the challenge, beginning with the initial contacts between institution and candidate, and increasing steadily during the course of the selection process.

It is our hope that what we have presented in this chapter will be of use to those interested in the presidency and especially the search process. As is apparent, much more than luck was responsible for the current successes of these schools—there are lessons to be learned from these individuals and their schools, and the analysis of leadership presented here can be a blueprint for others.

Warts and All— From the Other Direction

Admittedly, our discussion of these presidents has been mostly up-beat and positive, perhaps unnaturally so to some observers. However, our overall portrayals are justified by our findings in the field: These men and women simply *are* exceptional leaders.

Of course, they are not perfect; each has faults and critics, and several have been in serious trouble at one time or another. It seems appropriate to mention a few of their shortcomings. Definite problems were identified at most of these institutions, and the four most common ones were: confusion and bitterness regarding evolving standards for faculty; nonacceptance by faculty of an institution's strategic mission; mid-level administration frustration caused by presidential encouragement of end-runs; and presidential misperceptions about things such as their own visibilty on campus. The next most prevalent difficulty was probably campus concern about presidential consistency.

At institutions such as the University of Maryland and George Mason, standards relating to faculty appointments, promotion, and tenure have been dramatically elevated, to the consternation of some individuals who were pinched in the transition. At Maryland, John Toll arbitrarily and suddenly set standards at very high levels. While this did not concern all departments, some were infuriated and deeply resentful. George Mason's president George Johnson took a different tack, bringing in a cast of "superstars" and letting their presence dramatically raise faculty standards. However, his tactic was as unpopular in some departments at George Mason as Toll's was at Maryland.

The faculty who took issue with these two presidents actually focused on the standards themselves, rather than the process used to change them. Of course, in the end, Toll and Johnson had their way, as grudging compliance occurred.

Those closest to the presidents in our study were the people most knowledgeable and supportive of the leader's vision for an institution. We are convinced this was for two reasons: First, strategic plans are to a large degree created through an evolutionary process, and some faculty are seemingly never satisfied that the president has articulated his or her vision well enough; while on the other hand, those in on the ground floor, who can see what happens from the beginning, come to agree with the direction in which the college is moving. Also those in the mainstream are more enthusiastic about the strategic mission, perhaps for obvious reasons.

THE MANDARIN COMPLEX

Even dynamic institutions have their share of bureaucrats, and the academic kind are at times very concerned with things like chain of command. They dislike matrix management approaches. While the presidents studied did not cause significant disruption because of their tendencies to go directly after answers without regard to the organizational hierarchy and because they appeared to encourage shortcuts through the administrative maze, these practices are still resented by some mid-level administrators. If presidents do not accompany such unorthodoxy by trust-building within the administrative team, the results could be seriously disruptive to the institution as a whole.

CASPAR THE FRIENDLY PRESIDENT

Some good presidents have somewhat skewed perceptions of themselves compared to those of the faculty. For example, one president sincerely believed that he was quite visible on campus, but here is what the chair of his college council said: "He can't be serious. He's not visible, he's invisible. Why, when he gives that state of the college address in the fall, he does it with the lights off—a slide show." The gap between perception and reality is often a canyon.

WHO'S ON FIRST

In many of the institutions in this study, we perceived uneasiness about what the president might do next, and doubts about the consistency of his or her behavior. For example, at

Northern Arizona, Gene Hughes had been the model of consistency for years. He threw everyone a curve when he made the radical move to abolish the College of Education in 1983. This radical, perhaps opportunistic, change in a previously consistent president left many faculty with an uneasy feeling

Similarly, at Carnegie-Mellon, some faculty are nervous about . what Richard Cyert might do next. His proactive disposition, something in which he takes great pride, makes him suspect in some faculty circles, expecially the liberal arts faculty.

As is obvious, there are definite problems involved in even the most dramatically improved institution led by the most extraordinary president. The previously listed five difficulties were the most prevalent we found. In each institution, however, the positive tended to far outweigh the negative, and in many cases the same presidential qualities that made waves were eventually used to calm the institutional water.

CHAPTER 4

Trends in Administrative Practices

JOHN NAISBITT (1982) contends that by observing grass-roots endeavors, one can predict future national trends. Following his own tenet, Naisbitt's consulting organization reads hundreds of local newspapers from around the country to identify incipient trends. The resulting observations and predictions have proven accurate and valuable to educators, business leaders, politicians, and a broad spectrum of Americans interested in the future.

One of the benefits of our study of colleges and universities was the opportunity to observe practices at the grass-roots level among the 20 on-the-move institutions that very well may presage the future of American higher education. In the course of our data gathering, we identified the following prominent trends:

1. The use of initiatives as a strategic management tool is becoming common.
2. Three new power brokers are emerging on campus: the admissions, computer, and development officers.
3. Efforts to improve higher education are being instigated from the bottom up rather than from the top down.
4. High priority is being given to image building.
5. The institutional exploitation of alternate financial resources is increasing.
6. Traditional management structures are being dismantled.
7. An intense focus on quality is developing.
8. Attention to strategic planning is on the rise.

9. Increasingly strong relationships with business and industry are becoming common.

Some of these trends are appearing on the horizon and becoming generally recognized by many observers of the higher education enterprise. However, others, such as the use of initiatives as a strategic management tool and the rising institutional belief that responsibility for improving quality resides at the local institutional level, were phenomena we had not expected. These nine ground swell phenomena are delineated in the following sections.

The Initiative as a Strategic Management Tool

Time and time again, we saw well-defined projects being initiated to advance an institution as a unified whole. The type of initiatives we observed were ones that executed a strong pull on an entire institution. Such an institution-wide effect was achieved, we believe, because: (1) the positive image resulting from external publicity attracts resources from foundations, businesses, and federal and (in the case of public institutions) state governments; (2) a successful initiative excites and motivates people—students and faculty alike—throughout an institution, providing an example, building morale, and stimulating individual creativity; and (3) developing an initiative involves institutional self-assessment—a process that can refocus a college's attention on its environment and on its opportunities and advantages instead of its problems.

It appeared that institutions began using initiatives as a strategic management tool for one of three reasons: (1) the growing tendency of states to fund specific projects rather than provide across-the-board increases in budgets; (2) the fact that initiatives seem to be a natural outgrowth of strategic planning; and/or (3) simple desperation, the desire to get something started—a "try something . . . anything" philosophy.

For example, an administrator at the University of Maryland told us, "The only way we can get new money is through the selling of initiatives to the state. General nondescript increases are very difficult to get."

This point was reinforced by a 1982 *Chronicle of Higher Education* article entitled, "Supply-side Policies Have Come to Higher Education." The article posited that states would, with resources short and enrollments static or falling, steer higher education toward areas that might potentially provide a payback to the state economically or socially.

In many of the colleges in our study, we found a single major initiative had been pursued as an institutional focus, one that had an impact on the entire institution. For example, the development of the Center for Excellence in Education at Northern Arizona (NAU) was such an initiative (see Chapter 3). All of NAU colleges play roles in enhancing teaching excellence. Interestingly, this was not the first major initiative by an Arizona university. Several years earlier, Arizona State had achieved a major coup by getting Governor Bruce Babbitt and the Arizona industrial sector to fund a $30 million Center of Excellence in Engineering.

Northeast Missouri State University's (NMSU) value-added plan provides another good example of a single major initiative that yielded outstanding results in institutional pride, governmental relations, national recognition, and resource enhancement. The evidence is overwhelming—both candidates for Missouri's governorship in 1984 incorporated the NMSU value-added plan into their platforms, the state's higher education coordinating body designated the university as Missouri's state-supported liberal arts institution, and the legislature made a special $500,000 appropriation for the program; in addition, AASCU recently commissioned a book on Northeast Missouri's plan.

At some schools, such as Queens College, several coordinated initiatives were implemented, rather than a single large project. The core program in arts and sciences for women at Queens was only incrementally changed, while four peripheral initiatives brought additional resources, increased the college's visibility—locally and nationally—and ultimately restored the institution's self-confidence. The implications of the strategic use of initiatives by the management at Queens were profound.

Multiple initiatives were also in evidence at George Mason, DuPage, Maryland, Maricopa, Georgia, Tulsa, and other institutions. In each of these cases, multiple initiatives working in concert pulled the entire institution forward. At RPI, a major initiative included a capital project—a $30 million building for RPI's Center for Industrial Innovation, funded by the state and private industry, is now being built on the top of a hill at the center of campus. This dramatic structure is having a substantial impact on RPI's image as well as providing a financial and psychological enhancement for the programs to be housed in the facility.

Three New Power Brokers

After examining the data we accumulated on the final 42 universities we considered for our study, and the reports from our 20 field studies, we came to the conclusion that there are three administrators whose roles are being significantly enhanced on campus—the admissions officer, the computer expert, and the fund raiser. By power brokers, we mean individuals or division heads who have become extremely important on campus because of changing demographic and environmental conditions affecting higher education today.

Just a few years ago, admissions offices were to be found in obscure locations, cluttered with the paperwork of manual processing. Office decor was much like that of the registrar or the duplicating center, or other college backwaters. Those were the golden days of the baby boom when the major challenge for American higher education was coping with ever-increasing student demand.

Now the demographic landscape is quite different. The number of high school graduates has been dropping and the drop-off is predicted to be 25 to 30% over the next decade. Competition for students is now becoming formidable. As an example, an article in the April 3, 1985 issue of the *Chronicle of Higher Education* describes a virtual admissions war going on in Texas. Two Texas institutions were in our final pool—the University of Texas-Austin and Trinity University—and even though they were not visited for logistical reasons, it is quite evident that the competition between these two universities is very intense. Among other tactics, these two institutions are going after large numbers of National Merit Scholars with very attractive full four-year scholarships.

We found that admissions directors have now moved into offices which are well-appointed and prominently situated. Admissions publications are glossy and expensive productions; the latest electronic equipment of all kinds—VCR, videotapes, films, etc.—is part of the arsenal; and many admissions offices look like war rooms, with maps, charts, and graphs on their walls. In addition, the offices are now filled with cadres of young, articulate, well-dressed "admissions counselors."

Then, there are the ever-present computers. It seems that word processors and microcomputers have replaced typewriters. Computer terminals, tied to mainframes, or superminis, or minicomputers, are legion. Students and faculty are being enticed to acquire their own microcomputers with special deals. Hundreds of millions of dollars are being funneled into computer purchases, as campuses rush to be as up to date as budgets allow.

In the headlong rush to acquire computers, money is being wasted and mistakes are being made because of general ignorance. Persons with extensive computer expertise are in demand at both small colleges and major universities. The computer czar is becoming a new force on campus. Such individuals are highly paid, courted by everyone, and given prominent places on campus. Computing centers are no longer hidden in underground rooms, and if they are below the first floor, one would be hard pressed to classify their locations as basements. Everything looks more and more professional and businesslike, glass and steel and contemporary design combining to make the computer center a high tech shrine.

With the federal government diminishing its higher education funding and with state governments targeting their financial support more specifically, private fund raising is becoming increasingly crucial on campuses across America. As a result, development officers are becoming more important on campuses. Once located in auxiliary trailers, or in cubbyholes down the hall from the president's offices, development offices are acquiring lavish facilities of their own—for example, a spruced up president's former home at the edge of campus.

Computers, direct mail, and telephone marathons are in use practically everywhere: Higher education fund raising is big business today, and everyone on campus knows how important it is to institutional survival and enhancement. As a result, development officers are in prestige positions at both public and private institutions.

We noted that, contrary to their tradition, even community colleges are becoming interested in fund raising, with the local community college educational foundation concept spreading rapidly across the country. However, it seems community colleges as a rule are not looking for general support; rather, they are stumping for discretionary income to be used to fund special projects. In fact, a review of several community college presidential searches revealed a new development: candidates are now being asked about their knowledge of fund raising, corporate relations, and alumni organizations, areas usually extraneous to the community college president's functioning.

Bottom's Up—Innovation and Change Come from Below

One of the major trends John Naisbitt and his colleagues identified in American society in *Megatrends* was the movement toward a bottom-up rather than a trickle-down etiology for change. Naisbitt also identified a new entrepreneurial and innovative spirit afoot in America.

Both of these trends were also apparent among the 20 institutions on the move in our study. As if to underscore the reality of the first trend, we could not identify a single innovation, initiative, or success story among the schools we examined that originated in a state board of higher education. Most successful efforts to improve an institution, increase levels of quality, or serve students in any way were originated by one individual with an idea that attracted interest and support from other individuals, an institution, or outside concerns.

The Business and Professional Institute at the College of DuPage was initiated by President Hal McAninich; Rio Salado College at the Maricopa Community College District was created by Paul Elsner; the Center for Excellence in Education was conceived by Eugene Hughes. Presidents and chancellors, however, are not the only initiators on campus. The Tulsa curriculum was conceived by Provost Tom Staley and the Assessment Center at Clayton Jr. College has its origin with Linda Greer, Director of Research. Professor Paul Huray, Associate Dean of Liberal Arts and Director of the Science Alliance at the University of Tennessee, Knoxville, developed the Distinguished Scientists Program with the Oak Ridge Laboratories.

Conversely, we found state boards, offices, and bureaus to be the major obstacles to change and to improvements in quality, efficiency, and student service. This confirmed assertions of Peters and Waterman that inspector-generated quality improvement is virtually nonexistent and that rational planning by external agencies is usually negative, cautious, and nonproductive.

The Concern about Image

One of the things that appears to be sweeping through the American higher education system currently is the desire for positive feelings and beliefs about individual institutions. The lackadaisical approaches and attitudes of the 1960s are disappearing, to be replaced by a new emphasis on image, on the appearance of buildings and grounds, and on generally improving the atmosphere in which students live and learn.

Based on our studies, it seems that students are now increasingly attracted by a well-rounded campus identity, one that provides a good environment in which to spend four years getting a college education. Parents seem to be drawn to idyllic college settings for their children, perhaps in the nostalgic hope of recapturing something of yesterday's sense of place as a counterbalance to today's rootless society. We found St. Norbert College in Wisconsin to be a particularly fine example of this phenomenon.

While this parent/student attraction toward the idealized college is a traditional function of image, contemporary institutional concern with image goes beyond the usual ideas about the on-campus environment. This concern reflects a sincere and urgent desire to let the public know that college administrators are concerned with quality and are committed to addressing important societal issues (especially in the wake of the higher education reports of recent years). All of this may be motivated by the desire to ensure institutional survival, or by new measures of institutional success.

The Exploitation of Alternative Resources

Resource development has always been a primary goal of college administrators, but most usually focus on student fees, government appropriations, and private support—from alumni, foundations, and corporations. However, the institutions in our study, and an increasing number of others, are looking at new ways to develop different sources of financial support.

The varieties of alternative resource exploitation include entrepreneurial activities, initiatives into which some home business or organization can be enticed to buy, and simple opportunity consciousness. As America moves to a less regulated and more entrepreneurial society, colleges and universities will begin to look for new ways of enhancing their institutional resource base.

The pursuit of associated institutes, centers, and organizations that create a positive cash flow for an institution is a tactic that has been successfully exploited by Carnegie-Mellon, as witnessed by the creation of the Software Engineering Institute; by Maryland, with its National Bureau of Standards-associated Biotechnology Institute; and by George Mason, with its profit-making Instructional Television Fixed-Service (ITFS) telecommunications operation. In each of these cases, in addition to the positive cash flow generated, the reputation and quality of the institution was enhanced greatly, an additional benefit of inestimable value.

Some colleges have established training programs, "institutes" for seminars and conferences, and organizations serving business and industry tactics that also create a positive cash flow for an entire school. Examples include Queens College's New College and DuPage's Business and Professional Institute. These kinds of activities tend to serve real community needs, in addition to enhancing the image of the institution in its local community and providing alternative resources.

Other institutions are developing industrial research parks adjacent to campus on excess land, in the hope of creating an almost immediate cash influx and, in the long term, increasing the value of institutional assets (e.g., unused land). Examples include RPI Industrial Park building on university-owned land downriver from Troy, and Maryland's 600-acre Science and Technology Center, near its College Park campus.

The Erosion of Traditional Management Organization

Theories of organization, as taught in higher education programs and practiced in institutions, are being abandoned by presidents with new ideas who know that program development is critical to the future of colleges and universities. The standard practices such as "straight up and down the organizational ladder" and "hire specialists for every task" are increasingly being discarded.

This blurring of organizational lines and the use of alternative management structures has most probably come about for more than one reason. First, there is an increasing management tendency to try to use each individual's talents in a manner that complements the functioning of other individuals rather than attempting to superimpose a rigidly structured job on a worker. Second, higher education strategic planning, external pressures both societal and educational, and state and federal government priorities are combining to force college and university administrators to do things differently and more effectively.

At Northeastern Missouri State University, Charles McClain's management/administration structure for a 7,000-student university includes one administrative vice president and three deans—a virtually flat edifice. On the other hand, at Carnegie-Mellon Dick Cyert operates with two line officers—both provosts. Basic university operations, and the functions of departments such as those in the sciences, engineering, liberal arts, the libraries general research, student affairs, resource allocation, etc., are split more or less equally between the two officers. Such models are quite a deviation from the standard expectation of a president with a complement of four to six vice presidents.

At the two-year college level, the College of DuPage also has two provosts—one for internal academic operations and one for the external open college. The interesting thing about the operation of such institutions is how the president, through a unique structure, keeps his or her finger directly on the pulse of the school's academic/educational programs. No longer is the president a figurehead. Now, more than ever, successful institutions must be driven forward by better and more responsive educational programs, and it is becoming apparent that presidents must play a leadership role in this area. The president is having more "hands-on" experience; he or she is not relying exclusively on information to flow up from the ranks.

An Intensive Focus on Quality

There is a new emphasis on quality in American higher education. After a period of focusing on the schools in the wake of former Education Secretary Bell's report, *A Nation at Risk,* American higher education is coming under intense scrutiny. A number of reports have appeared during the 1983-84 and 1984-85 academic years, focusing on the quality of undergraduate education. All were critical of colleges and their faculties; at least one states that our colleges and universities are simply not good enough for the twenty-first century.

While the heightened interest in higher education of national organizations and the media is relatively new, we found that repairing the damages of the 1960s and meeting the challenges of the twenty-first century are processes that have been under way for some time at many colleges. Furthermore, the focus on quality has not been limited to the full-time undergraduate liberal arts student: institutional interests are much broader, including, in addition to the liberal arts, teacher education, science and engineering education, and the needs of adults and nontraditional students for a quality education.

For example, Northern Arizona University has made a major institutional commitment to improving its teacher education program. Alverno College, Northeastern Missouri State University, University of Tennessee-Knoxville, and Clayton Jr. College are involved in long-term commitments to value-added education. Bradford is moving forward in a major experment in the "practical" liberal arts.

At Carnegie-Mellon, RPI, the University of Tulsa, and the University of Maryland, there are carefully planned efforts to upgrade science and engineering by involving students in funded advanced research. We were particularly impressed with RPI's commitment to research for the sake of providing a better education for its students.

On the other hand, there is also widespread concern for providing adult students with a high quality education. Excellent examples of this concern dating back almost a decade can be found in Marylhurst and Aquinas colleges, where things have virtually been turned upside down to assure a first-rate education for adult learners. Community colleges, of course, have always been very committed to serving adult students.

Interest in quality goes beyond the curriculum, however. For example, attracting high-quality faculty is a priority goal for most of the institutions in this study. At Maryland, John Toll, to the consternation of some faculty and departments, has set very high standards for appointment, promotion, and tenure. At Tulsa and George Mason, major endowments are being used to attract leading academics. At Northeastern Missouri State University, Charles McClain has for over 10 years personally interviewed every serious candidate for a faculty position. In addition, several colleges in the group of 20 have faculty development programs.

Major commitments are being made to building high-quality facilities and acquiring the best computers and equipment. Colleges are accenting quality in their promotions and in student recruiting. While, of course, fueling healthy growth for colleges, the real beneficiaries of these trends across the educational spectrum will be the students of the next decades.

The Importance of Strategic Planning

As previously noted, strategic mission orientation was a dominant institutional characteristic among the 20 colleges we studied in the field, so it is no surprise to report that strategic planning is a growing trend among these colleges and universities. However, in looking at the 22 additional institutions on which we had accumulated files, and beyond these to other institutions, we discovered a keen and widespread interest in strategic planning as a discipline.

Institutions appear to have two common elements in their strategic plans: areas of specialization and marketing. Everyone wants to carve out a niche: Northern Arizona University and the University of Tulsa have launched major reforms in teacher education; Northeast Missouri State, Clayton, and Alverno have given institutional priority to the outcome of the learning process. George Mason aspires to distinction in the field of information technology. Bradford seeks to provide a unique curriculum and learning experience for undergraduates.

Institutions, too, are aggressively seeking persons interested in their new offerings. They are expanding their recruiting areas and developing new techniques to be used in their own "backyards." They are serious about meeting and beating the competition offered by other colleges. At St. Norbert College, for example, the message of total excellence in undergraduate learning is carried to prospective students by alumni, as well as admissions officers. With effective publications and public relations techniques, the college competes very well for students in the Chicago area, where high school seniors are faced with a multitude of options. St. Norbert has carefully identified their prime competitors and the things that attract students to those campuses. The college intends to challenge any competitior with attractive alternatives.

Billy Wireman at Queens College is a master tactician. He shapes public opinion with the nonstop message of Queens being exemplary. He convinces his community that the institution can uniquely serve their needs, especially in the adult market.

Much of this interest in specialization and marketing seems to have accelerated since the publication of George Keller's book, *Academic Strategy* (1983). Evidence of an even broader interest in strategic planning comes from two bits of information from George Keller himself. First, Keller has been employed as a planning consultant by over 200 colleges and universities since the publication of *Academic Strategy*. Second, most higher education administration books are fortunate to attract 3,000 purchasers, if the book is very popular, a second paperback printing may occur. However, *Academ-*

ic Strategy is now in its fifth printing. Academic strategy is becoming established as a discipline and a major administrative focus. George Keller has effectively spread the news to the far reaches of American higher education.

Strong Relationships with Business and Industry

One business leader told us, "Business is skeptical of college motives. For too long, they've (the colleges) operated on the principle of take the money and run. But now they are becoming more business-centered rather than totally self-centered. Cooperative ventures look a lot more attractive now."

Many of the colleges and universities in our study are developing productive relationships with businesses and industry. In Pittsburgh, Carnegie-Mellon is viewed as the major economic development resource; while at George Mason, a nonprofit corporation is sparking a broad array of industry-university interaction. DuPage has a highly successful business and professional institute; and at RPI, interaction with business and industry is the primary driving force in revitalizing the nation's oldest engineering school.

Over two-thirds of the 42 schools on which we have extensive files have developed important working relationships with business and industry. These efforts enjoy enthusiastic support in the private sector and help the colleges and universities in many ways. It is our belief this is a national trend.

While we make no claims to prophecy, these trends we have perceived among our 20 on-the-move institutions, and among the 22 other schools of which we made detailed analyses, seem to be acquiring lives of their own. In the larger higher education world, these may be the dogma of tomorrow: only time will confirm or deny.

CHAPTER 5

Ideas and Suggestions for Boards, Presidents, and Others

INSTITUTIONS, like individuals, are often very good at spotting the problems of others, yet can be the worst judges of their own troubles. The complex interweaving of the arcane and the mundane, intellectual rigor and pragmatic reality, and the myriad constituencies of a college, all combine to cloud perceptions on college campuses. It can be hard to figure out whether a college is on its way up, or riding for a fall. How do colleges and universities know if they are on the move? How can a board decide what type of leader will provide the spark needed to bring an institution to life? What steps should a president take to get his college on track?

Using the examples of our 20 institutions on the move we have formulated answers to these questions, which we have divided into four broad areas of concern: assessment of institutional movement; selecting a leader with the right qualifications and perspective; getting an institution moving; and suggestions for building "on-the-move" qualities.

Is Your Institution Moving?

In reality, we found that it is reasonbly easy to tell if a college is genuinely on the move, or if it is in deep trouble. However, it is difficult to give a prognosis when the institution is in the middle ground. In this regard, we believe it is very important for presidents and boards to acknowledge that their institution is simply treading water or stagnating—as hard as this may be—if this seems to be the case. To help in making such a determination, we identified pertinent indicators which appear to be important in determining if a college is healthy and advancing. These indicators are in the areas of strategic planning, students, faculty, resources, recognition, and leadership. Those interested in assessing their school should use the parameters outlined by these indicators to decide if the institution is healthy or in need of resuscitation.

INSTITUTIONAL WELL-BEING: SIGNS AND DEFINITIONS INDICATING AN INSTITUTION ON-THE-MOVE

1. Presence of a well-defined strategic mission. (A detailed definition, with examples of strategic mission, is presented in Chapter 3). This is simply a strong and deliberate declaration that is the basis for institutional planning and operating. It is important that this strategic mission be put into writing and that it be brief and understandable.

2. Strategic mission is well known. The mission must be understood both within the institution and externally and should be a document inviting internal discussion and involvement. Outside the college walls, the mission should appear in publications and speeches, forming the basis for institutional image building.

3. Strategic mission addresses relevant issues. The mission should address contemporary societal or educational issues such as improving undergraduate liberal arts education, upgrading teacher education, or building linkages with business and industry.

4. Financial resources are increasing in real terms. This is relatively easy to determine by comparing the increase of an institution's educational and general budget over a five-year

period to the consumer price index or the higher education price index.

5. External recognition is growing. Determining the degree of external recognition can be accomplished by reviewing newspaper clippings and other more or less independent publications. In addition, surveys in the community, reports of visiting committees, expressed interest of foundations, and other external indicators are helpful.

6. Number and quality of students is increasing. This can be determined by simply looking at five-year trends in applications, acceptances, and enrollees in the freshman class, along with a companion study of test scores, rank in class, and other criteria used for admissions decisions. In the case of open admissions schools new enrollee figures would be sufficient for analysis.

7. Faculty quality is improving. To determine if an institution is attracting a higher quality faculty, one can compare the credentials of those departing and of those arriving over a five-year period. Do those now at the college show more accomplishment and distinction? Is there evidence of more research and publication?

8. Faculty initiative abounds. Evidence of individual faculty initiative is very significant but may be difficult to assess, especially in large universities. It is important to note that both faculty perceptions and performances are of value here.

9. Strong proactive leadership is present. Such leadership can usually be identified subjectively, but it may be desirable to work through a more detailed and structured assessment if it is not abundantly clear that such leadership exists.

The use of these criteria represents the initial move: assessment. However, the one most crucial aspect of on-the-move progress is leadership. Choosing the hand to guide the wheel is probably the most important step in an institution's growth. The following section provides suggestions for those involved in the selection process.

Choosing a Leader to Move a College

*Academic strategy must begin with a change of heart and mind in the
academic executives—or a change of academic executives.*
(Keller, 1983:p. 165)

The one most crucial time when a governing board can
profoundly influence an institution's direction is when a new leader is to be selected. How does a board get the right match between its college or university and a president who has the qualities required to move the school to new heights (assuming the institution wants to move forward)?

It is necessary for those choosing a new president to be very
analytical with their college, blemishes and all, and with its future
possibilities. For board members, it is essential to look first at the
campus to determine its movement or the lack thereof.

For further assessment of an institution's identity, two options
are recommended. First, hire an outside consulting firm—prefera-
bly one with experience in academic strategic planning. Second, if
an instituion decides to have an internal review, the following
questions posed by Keller (1983:p. 121) should be considered as a
basis for assessment:

> Each institution needs to see itself as if for the first time and ask, What
> business are we really in? Of the 3,100 colleges, universities, technical
> institutes, seminaries, and two-year community colleges, what special
> role do we play in America's higher education network? What attrac-
> tive and important set of services does our institution provide that
> people cannot obtain elsewhere better, faster, or cheaper? What com-
> parative advantages do we have over approximately similar places?
> What academic fields and college services will be most needed by the
> country and our region in the next decade? With our traditions, en-
> dowment, location, and collection of faculty and administrators, what
> should our campus be building toward? What should our college as-
> pire to be 10 years from now?

Once a complete picture of the campus' current status and its
potential is obtained, then and only then should the board look for
a new president.

In choosing a leader, schools must work to avoid the pitfalls of common practice such as: forgetting about institutional needs and comparing individual candidates to one another, rather than to the school; looking for candidates who are complete opposites of the most recent incumbent; or favoring candidates who are most like a dearly beloved president who is the most recent, or a once revered leader.

To avoid these and other mistakes, we recommend a two-phase screening process for selecting a president. The first phase consists of the nuts and bolts questions and the assessment of general suitability for the office: deciding whether a candidate is a good administrator, a proven manager, etc.

Beyond these basic attributes our study revealed four unusual qualities that should be the exclusive focus of the second phase in a presidential search. These four qualities to be looked for in a candidate are: a parallel perspective relative to a college's current situation, educational leadership, energy and vision, and compassion.

IS A PARALLEL PERSPECTIVE EVIDENT?

A search committee or board must determine whether a presidential aspirant has the parallel perspective giving him or her a unique perception of the school. Candidates must simply be asked for his or her vision of the institution's future. What does this person consider special about the college—its programs, its location, its community, or its general situation—that gives it a competitive advantage over other schools in the 5 to 10 years ahead?

Answers to this question can tell much about the perspective of the candidate. Any responses should be a product of (1) knowledge of the school and (2) insight based on the individual's personal experience.

George Mason University president George Johnson told us of how he, as dean of the college of liberal arts at Temple University for 10 years, came to develop his own theory of what an urban university should be through pilot programs at the school. By observing Temple's successes and failures, and arguing with Temple president Marvin Wachman about Temple's mission as an urban college, this perspective was well developed when Johnson accepted the presidency of George Mason—and, he had the opportunity to test his vision at a fledgling urban university.

IS ACADEMIC INVOLVEMENT A HIGH PRIORITY?

Clark Kerr (AGB Reports, 1985: p. 24), in commenting on presidential leadership, said, "Too many presidents have withdrawn from academic affairs, been pushed out by faculty or pulled out by the pressure of external affairs. Presidents ought to be brought back into academic affairs. If presidents don't watch out for general education, nobody will."

In our study, all of the presidents were actively concerned with academic affairs. While there may be a natural and unofficial inclination on the part of faculty and others on search committees to want presidents who take a personal interest in educational programs, boards should insist that this be an official standard for candidate assessment. The question then becomes: Can search committees determine if a candidate will take an intense interest in academic matters, including the quality of educational programs?

Clearly, serving as a chief academic officer or department chair is not by itself sufficient evidence of academic leadership. In fact, a board should look for a combination of indicators: continued interest in working with students, including teaching; actual involvement with innovative programs; evidence of specifically allocating additional resources to strengthen critical programs; and raising funds from foundations and corporations to build up particular academic programs.

WHO POSSESSES THE ENERGY AND IDEAS?

The exceptional leaders of the 20 colleges that we studied were an energetic lot. Not only did they exude energy and spirit, but faculty, board members, staff, and others repeatedly commented on these leaders' vitality and creativity.

How does a search committee determine if a candidate has these qualities? Ask his or her colleagues, of course, and explore this question in depth in an interview with the individual under consideration. Ask candidates to provide examples of their own ideas and pet projects. Is there evidence of productivity? For example, one could easily identify Joel Read and Norbert Hruby as productive individuals, their résumés and support documentation would reveal feats that would take others much longer to accomplish.

What about their creativity? Do colleagues of the candidate know the person to be an endless flow of new ideas, as do Chancellor Paul Elsner's associates at Maricopa? What about the results of this creativity? There should be evidence of failures as well as successes; a fertile thinker with lots of ideas will have failures and should show evidence of having learned from their less successful ideas.

HAS COMPASSION BEEN SUFFICIENTLY DEMONSTRATED?

Again and again we found the leaders of these on-the-move colleges were compassionate men and women. We perceived this to be a critical balancing quality.

Harold Geneen (Schoenberg; 1985) may believe that people must have their heads knocked together to reach their peak performance level, but the leaders in our study got extraordinary effort from their people and were still considered compassionate. One might expect to discover hard charging devil-may-care presidents at the more aggressive of our on-the-move institutions: What we found instead were people who lead by example, and who were forgiving of those who, for whatever reasons, just could not keep up.

These leaders invariably put their schools first, but cared deeply about the people around them. We heard stories of presidents crying with subordinates whom they were removing from office, and of unexpected expressions of sympathy from a president to subordinates who thought that he or she was too busy to know about their personal problems.

We heard about a president who maintains a reserved facade in public, but who takes the time to write kind personal notes to staff members. If a recipient thanks him in public, the president will deflect the praise with light humor.

How can a board know that a potential president has the kind of compassion that an effective leader needs? Here are a few suggested techniques:

1. When asking candidates about some of their most important achievements and the reasons for their success, ask them whether other people were involved. Were other people helped? Is the candidate proud of the contributions and accomplishments of others?

2. Ask the candidate to describe one or more of the most difficult personnel decisions they have had to make. Do they express concern about the individuals involved? While making the best decision for their institution did they make an effort to accommodate the needs of the individual?

The four criteria we have highlighted as important for dynamic leadership are, most importantly, interdependent. Compassion without vision and ideas will not suffice; conversely, leading a college from one era to another will be costly in human terms, and must be done with care.

As fundamental as these characteristics are, they do not substitute for the basics—evidence of ability and interest in sound financial management, public relations, and general administration is essential for a candidate. However, many failed presidents have demonstrated potential in those basic areas as they moved up the ladder from college to college, but were incapable of leading an institution forward. More is required, and we think we have highlighted some of those essential, but rare, presidential traits.

Suggestions for Presidents, Advice from the Sidelines

Since we began discussing institutions on the move with people in higher education a tremendous interest has been expressed in just how one goes about getting a college moving. This was one question we were determined to explore, and we began by asking presidents for their views of the process.

What we found were three different approaches that seem to be situation specific. A number of presidents advised an incremental approach—start small and grow—while others favored campuswide changes made with alacrity. A third group advocated a process of laying out a grand but general design, then proceeding with specific steps in series or in parallel activities.

START SMALL

Charles McClain, based on his experience at Northeastern Missouri State University, advises presidents to start small, with voluntary groups, and then expand incrementally, even if the long-range goal is institution-comprehensive. His value-added education plan, after 12 years of small steps, encompasses the entire undergraduate program.

Many of the institutions we studied that had introduced major curriculum changes—such as Alverno and Clayton—have used this approach. It takes patience, perseverance, and a sense of continuity to make this strategy work.

HIT THE GROUND RUNNING

Arthur Levine brought both an idealized vision and a pragmatic plan to his presidential interview at Bradford College. He began implementation of both his first week on the job. Bradford was desperate for change and the selection committee, in effect, bet the institution on Levine and his ideas.

Eugene Hughes, in his sudden move to abolish the Northern Arizona University College of Education and replace it with the Arizona Center for Excellence in Education, struck at an opportune moment. By doing so, Hughes dramatically accelerated progress toward his stated goal of "building excellence one college at a time."

Major changes on short notice are possible, for example, by greatly altering delivery systems while leaving curriculum content relatively untouched. Literally overnight, Marylhurst College went from a liberal arts school for women to the Marylhurst College for Lifelong Learning. In a single faculty meeting, Aquinas President Hruby announced a completely new orientation for the college —age integration—along with a completely new administrative structure filled by named incumbents.

BREAK A LONG JOURNEY INTO SMALL STEPS

Undoubtedly at Marylhurst there was widespread recognition that environmental conditions dictated change, which prepared many for the announcement in the sudden fashion mentioned previously. However, when the campus situation is not generally perceived as requiring urgent action, faculty and others may resist dramatic moves. In situations such as these, we found presidents implementing a grand design plus an incremental-steps approach.

This was the case at Aquinas, where faculty incentive grants were made available and where an ongoing dialogue has been established to further define and refine the process of age integration.

Just as John Toll began to get settled at Maryland, he announced his overarching goal of turning his university into a top-10 public university, entering the company of such schools as Michigan, Berkeley, Wisconsin, and Texas. His first step was to raise promotion and tenure standards. Other steps followed.

Paschal Twyman at the University of Tulsa has set incremental goals for his institution, for example, in enhancing faculty quality. In this case, Tulsa is fortunate to have access to new money for development, which helps to facilitate the process.

DESIGN AND IMPLEMENT YOUR STRATEGY CAREFULLY

The first step in developing a strategic plan for a school is always forming an idea of the institution's future direction—a deliberate vision rooted in potential but balanced by reality. This vision will, of necessity, evolve; as the future unfolds, modifications and adjustments are essential.

Any strategic plan developed from this vision must contain several key components. It should be consistent with the institution's legal traditional mission, and it should address contemporary educational or societal issues (e.g., reorganizing university general education, upgrading teacher education, or building linkages with business and industry to improve the quality of education).

Once the strategy is to be implemented, all development efforts should be tied to this vision. This includes the traditional development areas a president must not be seen as just capitalizing on temporary public relations and fund raising. However, an effective strategy also depends on appropriate budgeting and staffing. The institutional rewards system, too, must tie into this plan. If it does not, then it will become easy for many to "sit this one out," thereby aborting any sense of mission.

As one president said to us, "It's like getting a snowball rolling—the problem becomes one of managing the process." To get some practical advice for presidents (and others) on how to control this process, we made special inquiries of several of our presidents.

Presidents Advise Presidents: The Quicksand of Campus Management

High Point College in North Carolina was strongly recommended to us as an institution that had turned itself around dramatically, and we looked at it closely.

Four years ago, High Point was in trouble: its president of 21 years had resigned; student applications were declining; and college relations with its affiliated religious denomination (Methodist) were not good. Faculty members became concerned about communication and administrative problems being left unaddressed.

Into this disorder came Charles Lucht, selected to turn things around as president in 1981. Lucht succeeded admirably. High Point had an increase in first-time enrollment in 1984; church-college relations are now positive; the college has developed promising relationships with the furniture industry in the High Point-

Greensboro area; and, in the fall of 1984, the faculty gave Lucht a strong vote of confidence.

One week later, the High Point board of trustees met and voted not to renew Lucht's four-year contract (it was due to expire in July 1985). Shortly thereafter, Charles Lucht resigned: He had failed to build a supportive relationship with his board.

The history of higher education is full of presidents enjoying major success but failing to forge a positive working relationship with one constituency—the board, faculty, or the external community. Even distinguished higher education thinkers such as Clark Kerr, who, in his words, "left the presidency of the University of California as I entered it—fired with enthusiasm," are not infallible when it comes to establishing a productive relationship with all constituencies.

Hanly Funderburk came to the presidency of his alma mater, Auburn University, after several successful years as chancellor of Auburn's campus at Montgomery. The new president had strong support from the board of trustees, the state legislature, and the alumni association. Funderburk launched a capital campaign and astonished everyone associated with the university by raising over $50 million. In addition, the Auburn athletic program, so important in Alabama, was dramatically improved.

However, Funderburk could never forge a positive working relation with his faculty, and after a series of confrontations with the faculty that threatened to paralyze the university, he resigned.

Effective administration is a fine art. Here are some pointers offered by the presidents we interviewed:

BUILD A MUTUALLY SUPPORTIVE RELATION WITH THE BOARD

The fostering of positive relationships with trustees can be characterized as a set of rules:

1. Always be honest with the board—to a fault. John Toll advises: "Work on a doctrine of no surprises."
2. Get to know the board members as individuals. What are

their interests? What are their strengths? Work with the chairman to get appropriate assignments for each trustee.

3. Recognize that the board has ultimate and total authority—but rarely exercises it. Boards are usually quite willing to allow much of their power to reside with the president. When they start pulling some of it back something is wrong, according to Charles McClain.

4. Never neglect your Board. Hal McAninch of the College of DuPage says, "You've got to always work at keeping a good relationship with the board." Boards change in many ways with time, and a negligent attitude toward board relations will almost certainly get a president in trouble.

Some interesting techniques were reported by the presidents to whom we directed our questions. For example, John Toll believes that "clarity in arrangements is a good thing. The board deals with policy, we deal with management, we're responsible to the board." Most of the presidents with whom we talked agreed with Toll. Although several cautioned that presidents should not try to dictate the arrangements: these must be negotiated carefully and clearly articulated.

Arthur Levine advises that presidents should be very candid about where they hope to take an institution as soon as possible—possibly even at their initial interview. Joel Read and Arthur Levine also believe that a new president must earn the respect of the board, by successful performance. In their opinions, if a president gets an institution moving in a positive direction the board will be very supportive—unless there is a fundamental difference in agendas.

There was also a strong consensus among the presidents that boards must have the best professional advice possible—even if they do not really want it at times. Sitting back and letting a board blunder into an embarrassing situation or working on an agenda separate from the board's is very dangerous for a president.

Harold McAninch strongly believes that "establishing that there is integrity among the administration is critical." He defined integrity as "not hiding anything, not being afraid to make an unpopular recommendation after you've looked at all sides of it, and that recommendation should be consistent with where you want to go."

Several presidents felt that bringing board members into the action is one way to give them a sense of pride, and make them more supportive. For example, John Toll said,

> We use our board members a lot. They have active involvement in the presentation of the university's case to the legislature.... Of course, it depends on the individual, but we've been fortunate. We've had people like Joe Tydings, former U.S. senator, as chairman of our board and they've been a great asset.

According to Toll, Tydings has talked to "editorial boards, Rotary Clubs, business groups, and legislative committees.... That kind of commitment from unpaid laymen is impressive to the legislature among others."

Joel Read advises that presidents must "get their own working style with the board." In other words, a new president cannot expect a board to relate to him or her in the same way that they did to a previous president; nor can a president expect to bring a set working style to a new position. Each board has its own personality, which must be understood and accepted by the president—incumbent or neophyte.

One piece of especially good advice we heard concerning working relations was: "Don't make things of small matter into things of great principle." This counsel should be applied when one is working with any university constituency—board, faculty, or external groups.

FIND OUT WHAT'S REALLY GOING ON

Alverno College's Joel Read spoke with us at length about the essentials to which a new president should direct his or her attention and energy.

> The first thing that a new president needs to do is find out what's really going on on campus. You should be careful, though, not to raise expectations. Those are tenuous times and it's easy to send mixed messages. You'd want to discover who the natural leaders are as well as who is officially in a position of responsibility....

Our presidents employed various techniques in keeping

abreast with the latest. Some stroll their campuses regularly, stopping to chat along the way. Chuck McClain meets regularly with students in the residence halls, cafeterias, etc. Eugene Hughes hosts frequent "hand shakers" where he can meet with faculty in a relaxed environment. Paul Elsner hosts employee meetings during which there is two-way communication with the classified staff. Norbert Hruby taps the campus grapevine and systematically "gathers intelligence." Because he is widely trusted, many people pass news along to him; he's careful, though, of what is to be taken seriously.

BUILD A TEAM, BUT ENCOURAGE THE INDIVIDUAL

As for building a team and a sense of group initiative, Arthur Levine had this to say:

> What I find effective is to share the kinds of problems that exist in the office, working with people in a collegial sense, not only sharing problems but also sharing solutions. . . . A sense of humor is important. I think four ingredients are important for team building: working together as colleagues on real problems, delegating authority to the group at some point, sharing humor, and, enjoying one another.

On the subject of team building, other presidents advised as follows:
John Toll—

> Mostly you want very able, bright people. Look for people who can't help themselves, both brilliant and compulsive.

Betty Siegel—

> It seems to me that you need people who can offer different perspectives. People who complement each other, and then you build a team on personal and professional diplomacy. . . . It's popular with some people to be the giant with all the pygmies around them, but the further I get along, the more I realize that a president should know his or her own limitations and get people around them to complement their strengths and weaknesses.

Harold McAninch—

> I've come in as president of three institutions and what I do is to look at the administrators who are there and see if they are willing to commit to where I want to go. I've found that most people are okay, with careful assessment and then explanation of what I want to do. I've not been required to change many people.

Advice on encouraging individual initiative on campus provided by the group included some shrewd and practical ideas. Betty Siegel told us,

> We're operating with very limited resources and what we say to people is, don't wait until we get the resources to do something. Try to find a way to do it better, more efficiently, more creatively, and then we'll do our darndest to reward you and to see that it grows. In the academic world, you have people who say, 'If I just had the money I could...' What we're saying is you have to be willing to make a leap of faith.

For a large university such as Maryland, John Toll suggests

> Your chairs and your deans are the key. They formulate the curriculum, motivate the faculty, and get things moving. Chairs have to, on the one hand, set high standards for promotion and tenure and, on the other, motivate the faculty to be creative in teaching and research. It's harder to get good academic leaders than it once was—the job's a lot harder today. So you have to figure out ways to help them. Stress how important they are to the university.

Harold McAninch stated that "the key is to let people pretty much be on their own. Talk to them, encourage them around goals that are institution oriented, and let them do it their own way."

KEEPING AN EYE ON THE COMMUNITY

A good working relationship with the external community is essential for any institution looking toward dynamic movement. While the external community varies for different types of schools, the advice to new presidents from our group of leaders worked out to be a fairly uniform set of rules:

1. Work outside of the office, as well as in it, accepting every speaking engagement received and soliciting others. This should go on for at least a year or two, with appropriate attention to all elements of the external community.

2. Bring community leaders to campus, encourage dialogue, then begin to create and interact. There are many opportunities to become active in community affairs.

3. Encourage staff to get involved in external affairs—speaking to groups and serving the community in a semicoordinated fashion. A president cannot bear the full weight of university diplomacy indefinitely, and shouldn't. A group effort by all the president's staff will be more effective, with the president becoming more selective in choosing his or her community activities.

4. It is very important to know what services the institution should, and can, provide to its external constituency. Do not assume that someone is taking care of this after a cursory examination of university-community relations has been made. Have an annual review, and try different tactics. Try to be flexible and prompt in providing what the community wants, where and when it wants it.

5. Finally, perhaps the most important thing to keep in mind—always be truthful to all external constituencies, from the legislature to the alumni association. In the words of one president, "A less than truthful answer can haunt a president for years."

The combined presidential experience of the six institutional heads whose responses formed the basis for this section totals 62 years. Not only are these men and women experienced, they are also successful, and it is from this experience and success that their wisdom flows.

Obstacles to Change

Finally, we heard a great deal about two of the thornier problems facing institutional advancement: Public colleges face the state bureaucracy; all institutions confront internal inertia.

THE STATE BUREAUCRATS

After a year of work, three universities in the Baltimore area—Morgan State, Towson State, and the University of Marylnd—had forged what they thought was a truly cooperative master's degree program is foreign languages. A worthy and long hoped-for goal was close to becoming reality. In order to get a degree from any one of the schools, a student was required to take at least six hours at all three: Each university would develop expertise in a special area. The plan would be cost effective, but more important, students in the Baltimore metro district would have the opportunity to pursue such a degree—an opportunity previously unavailable.

According to the story told us, this program was denied by the Maryland Board of Higher Education. The reason? It was not cooperative enough. According to the board, each diploma should have the names of all three universities on it. In shock, the cooperating institutions went back to the drawing board. The last report we had from Maryland indicated that these three institutions are still working toward getting a cooperative program started.

Northern Virginia Community College had a great idea in 1972. The school was going to be one of the first community colleges in the nation to launch an open campus. To be called the Extended Learning Institute (ELI), this open program would build a nontraditional campus around the delivery of courses by television and radio.

However, the Commonwealth of Virginia had other ideas. After going through several reviews by other agencies, the State Board for Community Colleges, and the State Council of Higher Education, Northern Virginia Community College finally opened the doors of the ELI—however, the ELI was two years late.

To deal effectively with state bureaucracies, it is necessary to understand their functioning and priorities. What are their concerns? As a group, state board staffs are apprehensive of mistakes. They are the consumate rational planners, as described by Peters and Waterman in *In Search of Excellence.* Making long-range projections, such functionaries always use the most conservative figures available and, combining a series of these, their final output is error consciousness geometrically compounded. Results can stray far from reality.

Higher education campus leaders should not expect much receptivity to innovation from state-board staffs. Our experience suggests they are antithetical to the process of change, and distrustful of those who are capable of innovation. A formula for having something new or innovative approved by a state board is, in our opinion, the following:

1. Always anticipate resistance and prepare for it.
2. Always figure out a way to allow state staffs to remain blameless if a plan doesn't work. They are definitely not risk takers.
3. Be persistent.
4. Be organized.
5. Figure out how an initiative or innovation will be cost effective, either now or at some future date.
6. Assess and consider the politics of the situation. Don't be naive.

THE CAMPUS STATUS QUO

Internal inertia is a natural component of most organizations, usually just a lack of interest in doing things differently, or in doing different things. In colleges this sluggishness often manifests itself in concerns such as: "Where is the money going to come from for this new program?"; "We could use the resources to make our program better"; or, "You can only divide a pie so many ways." The advice we heard from college and university heads on coping with institutional sluggishness included the involvement of faculty in a significant innovation. To use some specific ideas, Charles McClain urged fellow presidents to start big plans gradually, using volunteers. As an idea begins to take hold and show some success, a president should begin to expand and incorporate it into the institutional structure.

Betty Siegel advocates workshops and seminars to solidify opinion and direction. Most institutions undergoing significant changes develop a high level of intensity sooner or later; many institutions have a reward system for encouraging innovative faculty. Gradually, these factors soften resistance, and aid the unification process.

The suggestions and advice collected in this chapter represent the hard-won knowledge of 20 shrewd and successful presidents and chancellors, and the accumulated opinions of over 200 other campus functionaries. With victories far outnumbering defeats at their colleges, it is safe to bet that adapting their ideas will produce beneficial results.

Summary and Conclusion

We began the research for this book in an effort to understand what was happening in American higher education in the mid-1980s from a different perspective—that of outstanding, successful institutions. The research and prognostication of many regarding demographic trends and financial crises, along with the postulations of retrenchment, stagnation, and quality assurance via more state control, were well known to us.

We were troubled by the failure of leaders in American higher education to use insight such as Naisbitt's methodology to learn from evolving grass-roots trends in colleges and universities. Instead, we realized the tools of macroeconomics were being overused to define and then redefine the major national trend forces that will impact our system of higher education into the twenty-first century and beyond. The very theories and methods used to define the major trend forces were being used to justify major government intervention via the regulatory process—primarily at the state level.

Based on our readings and personal experiences, we suspected that something extraordinary was stirring at the grass-roots (institutional) level. We set out to discover if this were so, and if so, why some institutions were moving out from the threat of retrenchment, from relative stagnation, and on to new levels of effectiveness, excellence, and recognition. Rather than searching for excellent institutions and institutions that were maintaining excellence, we sought out institutions that were searching for a unique vision of excellence and that were enjoying a measure of success for their efforts.

We found that indeed there is an awakening at the grass-roots level—a fact demonstrated by the quick nomination of 112 institutions by a panel of 24 national figures in higher education. Had we pursued the topic, certainly a number of other institutions would have come to our attention. It was gratifying to identify (based on extensive institution-supplied data) 42 institutions clearly on the move. Of these, 30 were identified for potential field studies and finally 20 were visited. Using the Peters and Waterman approach, we looked inside those institutions and found some interesting trends, innovations, and common qualities.

The first overall conclusion that emerged is that these 20 institutions are people-oriented—caring, supportive, and nurturing. Indeed their primary focus is on people. This is evidenced by the necessity of having a strong leader with ideas whose role is acknowledged by the faculty and supported by a board of trustees. It is further apparent by our findings on the importance of teamwork, a shared vision, and individual initiative.

Nowhere, however, is the people orientation of those institutions more apparent than in their recognition of the importance of the customer—the student. The growing importance of the admissions/marketing officer, the intense interest in image, the preoccupation with quality, and the growing role of strategic planning with its emphasis on niches and comparative advantages all relate not just to the marketing of institutions but ultimately to students. Efforts such as alternative resource developing and fund raising for buildings, endowed chairs, and scholarships, are rooted in attracting students and giving them a good quality education. Furthermore, programs such as the value-added/competency-based education plans of Alverno, Northeast Missouri, the University of Tennessee at Knoxville, and Clayton Junior College, and experimental programs, the "Bradford Plan for Practical Liberal Arts," all focus on the student. In fact, practically every innovation, initiative, or plan in these 20 exemplary institutions was rooted in providing improved educational quality and opportunity—thus focusing directly on the student.

Another conclusion reported in this book is the failure of state regulating agencies to encourage new ideas. This finding only supports the earlier general findings of Americans that the government cannot regulate the nation into a dynamic economy and also the findings of people like Peters and Waterman that central rational planners tend to be cautious to the point of being negative. (We do not want to downplay the important role that governors such as Tennessee's Lamar Alexander are beginning to play. We refer here specifically to state coordinating boards.)

We found strong evidence of innovation, enterprise, and boldness at the individual level. To foster this spirit, direction, rather than detailed guidance and oversight, must be given. Encouraging people to take risks is important. As President Richard Ernst from Northern Virginia Community College stated: "It must be recognized that creative innovative people may sometimes fail in a particular undertaking—and such failure must be seen as an investment in the future of the institution. If failure is punished, nothing new or innovative will ever be tried."

We believe that this latter conclusion reveals a recommended course for state and national leaders if they truly want to pursue excellence in higher education and if they want the world's most marvelous experiment in education (American higher education) to be contemporary when America arrives at a new information age cultural consensus a decade or two from now. To maintain the overly rational bureaucratic approach so evident in many states will certainly retard the development of our colleges and universities relative to society in general—freezing many in the mentality of the transition period of the past two decades.

Our recommendation to government is simply this: Set the institutions free to pursue their own destiny reacting to the times, the market, and society in general. This means abandoning the posture of quality control by inspectors; the posture of preferring the retardation of some institutions supposedly to protect others; and the posture that wisdom is centralized. To do this the emphasis must shift from regulation based on macroeconomic trends to the encouragement of individual and institutional initiative. America's most precious resource is the minds of its best and brightest citizens. A healthy proportion of these "best and brightest" resides in America's colleges and universities. Federal and, especially, state authorities must abandon the view that initiative and even self-interest on the part of bright and entrepreneurial people are somehow bad. In fact, our only hope as a nation is to ensure that this creative energy is not only unfettered but encouraged! There are many approaches and many techniques, but the goal is clear and essential.

In summary, American higher education is on the move and this is good news. There is much which institutions and individuals can learn from one another and which people are willing to share. The question is, can the movement be accelerated? Will we be in time, considering the pace of change all around us? The answer to this question is a resounding "yes," if the innovations, initiatives, trends, and examples observed in the 20 sample colleges and universities reported in this study are part of a ground swell and not just isolated cases.

PART 2
THE INSTITUTIONS

Alverno College

Founded in 1887 by the School Sisters of St. Francis, Alverno College is an independent Catholic women's college located in Milwaukee, Wisconsin. Alverno was established as an institution aimed at preparing women for professional careers. In 1968 when Sister Joel Read assumed the presidency, the college was at the verge of collapse. Secularization had had a dramatic effect: enrollments had plunged, the capital outlay process was in disarray; there was a shocking absence of established policies and plans from the previous administration. When Sister Joel Read came into office, she met the challenge head-on. She "took the Board by the hand and taught it how to behave." Because of her strength and sense of direction, the institution recovered and now has become a nationally recognized model of distinction.

While Alverno has long been dedicated to "helping women develop their full potential," it has gained national recognition as an educational leader because of its impressive success with its ability-based curriculum, initiated in 1973. Alverno uses an approach to teaching and learning that focuses on each student's abilities and learning through practical experience, and the process is described as an "interplay of theory development and experience, reflection and practice." The students are heavily involved in an ongoing, active learning process and their progress is measured against eight abilities that each student must eventually master: critical thinking, problem solving, communication, social interaction, valuing, environmental responsibility, civic responsibility, and aesthetic response. The teaching and learning process involving these dimensions is developmental and interdisciplinary since the eight abilities are stressed in all academic courses. Two critical components of the ability-based approach to education at Alverno are assessing how well a student applies skills learned and evaluating the effectiveness of Alverno's total program.

In 1977, Alverno instituted a "Weekend College" program based on the same educational philosophy. The Weekend College stresses the ability-based approach to learning and adds a special convenience: students can earn a college degree by attending classes every other weekend. Most students in Weekend College are locally employed. Since the program began enrollment has increased from 250 women the first semester to almost 900 in the 1984–85 academic year.

Alverno College's total enrollment in the fall of 1985 was 1,513 students, the highest enrollment in the college's 98-year history. Alverno's 35 program areas are contained within five academic divisions: integrated arts and humanities, behavioral sciences, natural sciences and technology, fine arts, and nursing. Half of Alverno's students are Catholic, and 60% come from the greater Milwaukee area. In the day college, two-thirds of the students are under the age of 23; in weekend college, two-thirds are under 32. About 80% of Alverno's students receive some kind of financial aid.

The results of Alverno College's programs are striking: Within six months of graduation in 1983-84, 93% of its graduates were employed (virtually all of them in the fields for which they prepared at Alverno).

In the areas of research and community service, Alverno has completed a seven-year study funded by the National Institute on Education focused on outcomes of the education program and career effects after college, published a book on teaching communication skills across the institution's curriculum, organized a national network of teachers interested in critical thinking abilities, and prepared more than 100 consultations and presentations for other colleges and organizations.

Alverno has received its share of national attention: The school has been named one of the best small colleges in the midwest and west and one of the three most innovative nationally in a survey of American college presidents completed by *U.S. News and World Report;* Alverno was one of five Wisconsin colleges selected for the *New York Times* "Selective Guide to Higher Education"; and in 1984, the college was chosen to take part in a national leadership training program led by the National Executive Service Corps and the National Association of Bank Women. In addition, Alverno was recently chosen to receive an outstanding education program grant by the Exxon Educational Foundation.

Perhaps one of the most distinctive characteristics of Alverno College is its commitment to women. Reaching beyond the classroom, the college has created a Research Center on Women "to provide the setting and impetus for women to seriously examine their own status, to identify and understand the many historic and contemporary forces that have determined that status, and then to create the desire and devise the strategies by which women, with assurance and self-respect, will lead the way toward requisite social change."

Alverno College is as unique as its President. Joel Read clearly believes in diffused power on campus. Decision making is highly collaborative; there are many faculty-staff committees and a myriad of meetings. Sister Read, however, is aggressive in this group process. She continually throws out new ideas to her colleagues, some of which are not well-received. When she attempts to influence the decision-making process, disagreement does occur. In spite of Joel "ruffling a few feathers" it is clear she is a catalyst which keeps the organization exciting and rewarding.

While Sister Read is an accomplished administrator, she also is a scholar, with specializations in the learning process and the women's movement in America. Her intellectual prowess is evident in her managerial style. She digests literally every bit of information that's circulating at the college (faculty minutes, reports, etc.) As a result, she is in command of an impressive array of knowledge and is always abreast with the latest happenings.

Aquinas College

Aquinas College, Catholic in its tradition, is independent in its control. Established by the Dominican Sisters of Grand Rapids in 1922 as Sacred Heart College, the school was renamed Catholic Junior College in 1931, at which time it became coed—the first Catholic coeducational institution in the country. In 1941, the college became a degree granting institution and changed its name to Aquinas. It moved to its present location, a 70-acre turn-of-the century estate, in 1945. (Aquinas, considered by many to have the most beautiful college in Michigan, has on its grounds examples of almost every type of tree and shrub, some 120 species, that can grow at that latitude).

In 1969 it appeared doubtful that Aquinas would survive

another five years. Despite the quality of the college, hard economic times had hit all small church-related liberal arts colleges. Aquinas, like many other small Catholic colleges, had retained unrealistically low tuition rates and the education of the students was heavily subsidized by the Dominican Sisters who donated their time and the Dominican priests and lay people who worked for substandard pay. Most of the "old timers" at the school do not believe Aquinas would exist today had it not been for Norbert J. Hruby.

Hruby accepted the presidency of Aquinas in 1969 "on condition that the college enter immediately upon an intensive inductive institutional self-study in the belief that the attainment of educational excellence is not possible without thorough, accurate, and objective self-knowledge. . . ." The self-study, which Hruby describes as his "entry tool," was organized around the prospective student's life and work. Aquinas, according to Hruby, realized that it "must serve the student as though he or she were a customer rather than a captive."

As a result, Aquinas under Hruby inaugurated a number of programs specifically geared toward nontraditional students, adult and continuing education, community outreach, and career preparation, including the programs listed below.

> Career Action—An evening degree completion program in business administration for employed men and women.
> Encore—A daytime degree completion program for women over the age of 26.
> Veterans Counseling—A special admissions and counseling program assisting the veteran in adjustments to college.
> Summer School Without Walls—An independent study program involving contractual commitment between student and professor.
> Survival Skills Center and Student Tutoring Service—A service designed to help students who have college potential but need assistance in basic study skills.
> IDEA—An external degree completion program consisting of "independently designed education for adults."
> Eastown—An experimental program, funded for three years by

the W. R. Kellogg Foundation, for improving the quality of
life in a 72-block neighborhood adjacent to the campus.
Emeritus College—A program of noncredit liberal arts classes
for retired persons offered at the college and at area retire-
ment homes and. churches.
Career Development Center—An organized program of career
preparation, for freshmen through seniors which encompasses academic advising, courses, counseling, field experience, and job placement.

Hruby believes that the end of education is to prepare people to
cope with a world in rapid, radical, discontinuous change. He
believes that teaching and learning are the means and that learning
is far more important than teaching. He also believes that the best
leader is a broker, a catalyst, a key participant in the learning process shared with the student.

Given this philosophy, Hruby does not believe that anyone
leading an educational institution can be manager or caretaker or,
indeed, anything other than an entrepreneur. This, according to
Hruby does not necessarily suggest a kind of academic Iacocca, but
it does suggest an educational leader who has imagination, aggres-
siveness, foresight, prudence, integrity, and more than a little bit of
luck.

On February 3, 1984, the fifteenth anniversary of his presidency
at Aquinas, Hruby delivered a strong "state of the college" address
to the faculty. He described a thriving Aquinas with the largest
student body in the history of the college, a first-rate faculty, a competent and caring administration and staff, an improving physical
plant, a balanced budget, and a growing endowment. He set that
picture within the national context of higher education in a "steady
state" facing an increasingly serious enrollment crisis. The standard
institutional responses to adversity, according to Hruby, are all
reactive rather than proactive. Hruby said, "I believe there comes a
time in the life of an institution when, no matter how secure it is, or
believes itself to be, it must nevertheless be pro-active rather than
reactive. . . . and I believe that time is now." Hruby concluded that
Aquinas should "press ahead to become that subtly but substan-

tially different type of college—namely an age-integrated college." The college would retain its mission but no longer maintain its "separate but equal" treatment of its older and younger students. "If we are to be truly integrated, Aquinas must have one administration, one faculty, one curriculum, one schedule, and most importantly—one student body." Hruby explained that having "entered continuing adult education fifteen years ago with a sense of mission, we may have overcompensated. By giving special attention to the older student—for which we certainly do not apologize—we may have created some inequities for the younger students."

The administrative structure of Aquinas has been changed to implement age-integration, and the college is now engaged in strategic planning. Task forces are currently studying, among other topics, tuition structure and calendar and course formats. A number of faculty incentive grants (FIGS) have been awarded to faculty to study "the new kinds of pedagogy implicit in an age-integrated college."

Recently Hruby wrote to his faculty,

> When I was a kid, I wanted to be a champion of something, but I never had the talent or the strength. But now as a sexagenarian ... I have found a second meaning of the word *champion*. I have become a champion of the non-traditional student. More importantly, Aquinas College has become the very special champion of the non-traditional student, for it has *welcomed* men and women of every age, ethnic background, race, religion, and physical condition. It has done the right thing for the right reason. It has been not merely reactive but proactive, not self-serving but serving. That is the true mark of a champion college.

Hruby also has done the right thing for the right reason—the mark of a champion president.

Bradford College

Bradford College is a private, four-year liberal arts college located in Haverhill, Massachusetts, just north of Boston. Established in 1803 as a coeducational academy, Bradford became a women's secondary school in 1836 and eventually became a junior college for women in 1932. Since 1972, Bradford College has been a coeducational institution offering both bachelor's and associate degrees, with a current enrollment of approximately 425 students from 25 states and 30 foreign countries.

Bradford entered a period of adversity in the late 1960s as outside support and enrollments began to slip. Going coed and finally moving to four-year programs were efforts to broaden the college's base. It quickly became apparent that this was not enough as the changes did not increase enrollments very much while the four-year curriculum required substantial additional resources. By the late 1970s, Bradford was in turmoil. The college was running deficits and the faculty was in open revolt. The institution desperately needed a new direction. It was ready for a new and different leadership style.

With the appointment of Arthur Levine as president in 1982 Bradford took a bold new direction, creating its Bradford Plan for a Practical Liberal Arts Education, "A program that combines Bradford's historic tradition of quality liberal arts education with a desire to prepare students practically for life after college." Bradford College offers a practical liberal arts education that addresses what the institution considers to be the five basic needs of American education: (1) to upgrade student basic skills; (2) to rethink general education, the learning that should be common to all people; (3) to provide students with better career preparation; (4) to reaffirm the importance of ethical values and social concerns; and (5) to respond to changing demographic, financial, and social conditions.

The Bradford plan is a curriculum composed of seven principal elements: basic or communication skills, general education, freshman inquiry, a comprehensive major, a liberal arts minor, a liberal arts internship, and junior and senior projects.

In the area of communication skills, the college notes that "every student should learn the basic languages human beings use to communicate: words and numbers. They need to learn how to use them—speaking and writing. And they need to understand how to interpret them—reading, listening, and seeing."

General education focuses on "those experiences that knit isolated individuals into a community," and encompasses seven broad areas of study: the shared use of symbols, shared membership in groups and institutions, shared activity of work, a shared global perspective, a shared relationship with nature, a shared sense of time, and shared values and beliefs.

Freshman inquiry is an annual event during which each freshman is required to write a 1,500 word essay on his or her freshman year, current intellectual identity, and future academic plans. Each student meets with an advising team (composed of faculty, administrators, and another student) to evaluate the essay and academic plans.

A comprehensive major is education in a specialty area that must meet three criteria: the major must be a discrete and coherent body of knowledge, it must employ accepted ways of knowing, and it must teach higher order intellectual skills.

The liberal arts minor is a "mini-major, a four- to five-course sequence of classes with a common theme," which allows the construction of a skill area or field of expertise such as communications, gerontology, or human services.

The liberal arts internship is "credit bearing, short term, supervised learning in an out-of-class, usually off-campus, setting."

The senior project is the "capstone to a baccalaureate education" at Bradford; it provides for the application of skills and knowledge learned at the institution "in the solution of an academic or creative problem.... In this sense, the senior project marks the transformation of the undergraduate from a dependent to an independent learner."

The junior project is a course designed to take students through the senior project exercise. As a group, a class works together to find a solution to a problem identified by the faculty member assigned to the course.

Instituted by Arthur Levine, the Bradford plan has received national attention for its innovative approach to liberal arts education: student inquiries have more than doubled, and applications have increased 34%. The potential of the Bradford Plan as a curricular model brought $232,000 in grant monies during 1984 from the Fund for the Improvement of Postsecondary Education, the Exxon Education Foundation, the Surdna Foundation, and the Alden Trust.

The Bradford Plan for a practical liberal arts education is a unique initiative that has been received with great enthusiasm by the entire college community. In the words of President Levine, "The Bradford plan is a means of ameliorating the difficult demographic and financial conditions all colleges, especially liberal arts schools, face." Levine not only sees the Bradford plan as a means by which the college can produce a first-rate graduate, but also the means by which Bradford College can truly thrive. "Throughout its history ... Bradford has continuously evolved to meet the ever-changing needs of American society. The Bradford plan is a blueprint for meeting those needs well into the 21st century."

Arthur Levine is the youngest president in our 20 example institutions and perhaps the most unconventional. By unconventional we are referring to the fact that Levine jumped from a senior fellow at the Carnegie Foundation for the Advancement of Teaching to the presidency at Bradford without holding any significant prior academic positions; his unique curricular perspective on general education and the liberal arts, which is the primary force now driving Bradford; and the fact that while Levine has inserted his ideas on curriculum into Bradford and has been phenomenally successful in writing, securing funding support, and maintaining a national presence, he has tinkered only moderately with the administrative staffing and functioning of Bradford.

Levine is a man of strong convictions and drives the curricular reform under way at Bradford by his ideas and personality. He sees Bradford as an experiment of great significance to the future of American higher education. The Bradford College community has bet its future on Levine and his vision.

Carnegie-Mellon University

Carnegie-Mellon University (CMU), located in Pittsburgh, was founded in 1900 by steel magnate Andrew Carnegie. Originally named Carnegie Technical School, the institution became Carnegie Institute of Technology in 1912, and in 1967, after merging with the Mellon Institute of Research, Carnegie-Mellon University came into being.

In 1984, CMU enrolled 5,600 students, with 1,500 in graduate programs, in six colleges. The engineering college and graduate school of business are ranked in the top 10 nationally, and its computer science department (the first in the nation) is on a par with those of MIT and Stanford according to defense department research officials and others. CMU also has a commitment to excellence in the arts and humanities. (In fact some criticize the university for its efforts to be excellent in two diverse fields.)

The university has enjoyed a rapid rise to national recognition in the past 25 years. Carnegie-Mellon University has been featured in a wide variety of publications, from George Keller's *Academic Strategy* to *Business Week* to New York Times editor Edward Fiske's *Selective Guide to Colleges 1984-85,* where CMU is characterized as "evolving from a superb regional to a national institution." Fiske comments on the university's success and originality "in pursuing the twin goals of liberal-professional education."

The following quotation by Fiske describes CMU's approach to general education in one of its colleges:

> Students in the College of Humanities and Social Sciences follow a new and imaginative core curriculum of nine specific courses designed to equip them with a "portfolio" of high-level intellectual skills. The core curriculum emphasizes an ability to transfer knowledge from one field to another, and a student taking a final exam in a social science course may encounter a question on a book assigned in a literature course. Having these students take at least nine courses in common reflects the university's belief that not all education takes place inside classrooms; modified versions of this core are being introduced in the other schools. As Herbert Simon, the Nobel Prize-winning economist who helped design the core curriculum, states it, 'We want to provide some common topics of conversation besides sports, the weather, and sex.'

Carnegie-Mellon University works at being on the cutting edge of educational developments. For example, in 1982, it declared its intention that each student should have his or her own microcomputer—tied to a campus network. This first-in-the-nation innovation is being carried out in a joint endeavor with IBM and is expected to cost $50 million by the time it is completed.

In late 1984, the Defense Department announced that CMU

had been chosen as the location of its defense department sponsored $103 million Software Engineering Institute (SEI). One has only to recognize that the discipline of software engineering is barely a decade old and that the Software Engineering Institute is the nation's first major software engineering research effort to comprehend CMU's national stature in the computer science field. (Most major advances in the use of computers, e.g., timesharing, came out of defense and space exploration efforts.)

These developments did not occur overnight, but in the higher education community, with its general resistance to change, the CMU story does not seem unusual. However, CMU's evolution into a top national institution has not been without its crises and difficulties.

Beginning with the Carnegie Plan of President Robert Doherty in the 1940s, CMU moved steadily toward becoming an outstanding regional university by becoming more selective in admissions, emphasizing research and getting some of its programs recognized nationally. However, during the mid-1960s the school entered an era of uncertainty, as the turbulence of the Vietnam years, a lack of leadership, and the decline of the steel industry clouded the future of the school.

By 1972, CMU prospects were diminishing despite two decades of growth and development. Sizable operating deficits had begun to accumulate, and in 1972, CMU found itself in a financial crisis. Furthermore, despite the quality of several programs, considerable confusion existed as to the university's future direction.

Then Richard Cyert, the dean of CMU graduate school of industrial administration, was appointed president. Cyert early in his administration developed three initiatives. First, he took firm control of the fiscal management of the university, integrating sound management principles into academic practices.

Then he began an effort to build an atmosphere within the university that encouraged individual initiative, an effort initiated by the establishment of a mini-foundation on campus to fund innovative educational programs.

Finally, Cyert developed a strategic plan to lift CMU to a position of national recognition. Traditional academic wisdom holds that an institution can be changed by changing the faculty, *or* the students, *or* the curriculum, but that it is risky to attempt to change more than one.

Cyert set out aggressively to do all three. First, he instructed all departments and schools to look for "niches" where the university could carve out a role for itself and for eminent faculty who might be attracted to CMU. As the departments and faculty developed, Cyert pushed nation-wide student recruiting—in the process, changing the institution's base to more of a national one.

Thanks in large part to this plan, CMU has been repeatedly honored for its strategic planning, and has become something of a model for colleges and universities all across America. In addition, Richard Cyert has been widely recognized for dramatically raising CMU to national stature while becoming something of a legend himself.

Cyert is a nationally recognized authority on organization and we asked for some of his thoughts on leadership in higher education. Some of his observations are:

> Leadership in decentralized organizations such as universities must be exercised through many different means of communication. The president's behavior in relation to research, teaching, new ideas, or working habits is an important aspect of setting the desired tone in the university. The president must find ways of communicating directly to individuals, to small subunits, and to the faculty and staff of the university. The president must be prepared to communicate orally, in meetings, and in seminars as well as in writing. He must use all methods of communication and all types of forums to get the message across to his constituencies. This message must relate to the goals of the university. These goals must be set for the university with the participation of the faculty. . . .
>
> Strategic planning requires the organization to make an analysis of its potential comparative advantages. Each department in the university should be constructed on a base of comparative advantages. There are many types of comparative advantages that an institution may have. Some may stem from history, others from strength of different departments within the university, and still others from individuals within a department. Occasionally, a comparative advantage may stem from location. . . .
>
> A university has two major goals; one, the dissemination of knowl-

edge and the other, the creation of new knowledge—research. The research goal is more consistent with faculty desires. Since excellence in teaching is a critical goal for the university, the president and central administration must expouse it. The president must take action to insure that the attitudes of the faculty toward teaching are positive and consistent with the desired goals of outstanding teaching. . . .

The president must be capable of getting into the details of all aspects of both the academic and non-academic administrative requirements of the university. The president must be capable of leading the university through developing a set of attitudes on the part of faculty and staff that is consistent with the achievement of the goals established for the organization. In addition, the president must develop planning procedures so that each department in the university is building on its comparative advantages. In that way, the university is strengthened at its base.

Clayton Junior College

Clayton Jr. College, founded in 1969, is a part of the University System of Georgia serving south metropolitan Atlanta. Clayton's location is clearly one of its driving forces. Atlanta, the hub of the southeast, is one of the fastest growing cities in the country. Clayton's beautiful campus is situated on a 163-acre tract of land that includes three lakes.

Clayton was established to provide educational opportunities for the community within commuting distance of the college. When it opened in 1969, Clayton had 942 students and approximately 35 faculty members. In the two decades from 1960-80, Clayton County's population expanded from 50,000 to over 150,000, and today the county has approximately 165,000 residents. The college now has approximately 3,400 students.

Approximately 45 college transfer programs are offered at Clayton, including the traditional liberal arts and preprofessional programs. In the Division of Vocational Technical Education, the college offers about 16 one- or two-year programs, including data processing, drafting and design technology, electronics technology, management and supervision, office administration and technology, and medical laboratory technology. Other two-year programs such as nursing, dental hygiene, and aviation administration are also offered.

President Harry S. Downs was a member of the staff of the Georgia Board of Regents for nine years prior to assuming the presidency of Clayton. As assistant vice chancellor on the board staff, Downs had been responsible for junior college development. At the time he was given this assignment, four junior colleges had already been approved, but only three were under development. Downs had the opportunity to plan and develop the approved but undeveloped institution from its inception, using existing computer programs to simulate its operation, thereby projecting the specific facilities (i.e., classrooms, laboratories, faculty offices) needed. He also decided to use modular building techniques and a computer-assisted central path method in the design and construction process. These three elements had not previously been combined in the development of a single institution, and the Educational Facilities Laboratories awarded a grant to the project. The result, Macon Jr. College, was successful, and consequently, Downs used the same approach to develop Clayton Jr. College.

Another assignment that Downs had been given while on the Regents' staff was to find a solution to the problems of transfer credit among University System institutions. This assignment resulted in the development of the core curriculum adopted by the Georgia University System in 1967. Because of his work on the core curriculum and junior college development, Downs had spent considerable time studying general education. While Downs did not have a fully developed concept of what general education should be, he had some strong ideas of what it should *not* be—and an even stronger feeling that "we should at least say what it is we expect the outcomes of general education to be." Downs has long believed that "the heart and essence of higher education is the learning process; the interaction between students and faculty that results in discovering and rediscovering the joys of learning and becoming efficient lifelong learners." Downs firmly believes that *all* other facets of institutions must be justified in terms of their support of the teaching/learning process, or of their direct support of research and service functions.

Now in his sixteenth year at Clayton, Downs is beginning to see some of his ideas concerning general education become realities. The major thrust at Clayton College is the development of an outcome-focused, assessment-based general education program. The faculty initially identified eight desired outcomes of general education in two general categories: Skills—communication, critical thinking; and Perspectives—esthetic, contemporary, historical, mathematical, scientific, and value-oriented. Councils have been established for each of the eight outcomes, and these groups are working to achieve consensus on the goals of general education at Clayton, including determining how to measure whether a student has achieved the objectives.

Another important thrust at Clayton is continuing education. Business and industry are booming in Clayton County, and Downs strongly believes that junior colleges in urban communities exist to *serve* the community. One of his goals is for Clayton to be an integral part of the community. He believes that individual faculty members should serve as contributing citizens to the ongoing process of improving the quality of life of the community, and he encourages all faculty to become involved in the community and to contribute to its development. Local residents, including many people who have never attended any college, speak with affection of "our college." A resident whose son graduated from Clayton several years ago said, "It is the kind of school that you are proud to have a child attend." She went on to explain that faculty are genuinely interested in the welfare of the students and that the college is interested in serving the community.

Residents of the community are welcome on campus at any time. Particularly in the spring many people fish in Clayton's lakes, jog on the roadways, or simply stroll around the 74 acres of the campus that have been left in their natural state.

A senior vice president of the National Bank of Georgia said concerning Downs,

> He has been 'our' president since the college opened, and he is one of our most outstanding citizens. The thing that is different about Harry is that he assumes roles in the community much different from the 'ceremonial leadership roles' that so many college presidents assume.

He is a worker. This is *his* community and he is involved in it. He has been instrumental in helping us (the Chamber of Commerce) get some very difficult things done.

Concerning the college, the bank officer said, "The college is well respected by the community, and I personally am thrilled to death with it as a citizen." He went on to say, "It is not too strong to say that we would not be competitive today in metropolitan Atlanta had not the college, and specifically, Harry Downs, been here."

College of DuPage

The College of DuPage began operation in 1967 as a state-affiliated community college with an initial enrollment of 2,621 students. In the last 17 years, the college has experienced a very high rate of growth, currently with approximately 1,400 full- and part-time faculty and almost 30,000 students. The main campus is a 273-acre site in Glen Ellyn, a suburb of Chicago, and the college operates 80 off-campus satellite centers scattered throughout the college district that serve a population of over 700,000 (including 23 public high school districts, eight parochial high schools, and 42 municipalities).

DuPage recognizes the need for community colleges to serve both nontraditional and traditional students, and has acquired a reputation for its ability to serve both groups well. Harold D. McAninch assumed the presidency of DuPage in 1979, shortly thereafter creating two institutional components: Central Campus and Open Campus. This reorganization of the traditional institution was implemented to (1) seek innovative ways of meeting current challenges facing education; (2) investigate methods to more effectively meet the mission of a community college; (3) establish a sound base of community support; and (4) identify new markets and new audiences. The Central Campus is responsible for traditional degree and certificate programs (both credit and noncredit) in nearly 80 prebaccalaureate areas of study and over 40 occupational and technical programs. The Open Campus is in charge of "taking the college to the community," and offers flexible learning opportunities through film and video and audiotapes, textbooks, independent study, radio and television classes, weekend degree programs, and "Alpha One," a travel-learning program. In addition, the college has many programs for specific target groups, including senior citizens, women, and children.

Most of the DuPage students come from the local community (business, industry, professions, homemakers, etc.), with 28% coming from local high schools and another 7% enrolled as reverse transfers. DuPage is proud of the student population age range, from 16 to 90 plus years (average age is 30). DuPage has undertaken follow-up studies of its students and reports that as of 1984: (1) 87% of transfer students attend Illinois colleges and universities; (2) approximately 49% of students who receive associate degrees transfer to public institutions and 51% select private colleges; and (3) one year after graduation, 64% of the college's graduates found employment within the college district and 79% were employed in a field related to their course of study.

The College of DuPage's Business and Professional Institute (BPI) is a successful cooperative venture with business and industry which was conceived by President McAninch. Recognizing the opportunity provided by the college's location in a rapidly growing high tech corridor, the BPI was established in 1979 to serve the educational and training needs of area businesses and professionals, and is a self-supporting operation. Some of the programs provided by the BPI are education, training, and economic development assistance to businesses, in addition to practical programs designed to improve the skills of professionals, programs for assisting in-plant closings and major technology shifts, and retraining opportunities for the recently unemployed. The Regional Assistance Center was so successful during its first year of operation that the college has received a second $500,000 state grant to extend the operation for another year, and is now assisting the displaced employees of approximately 30 plants in making the transition from unemployment to new jobs.

In the area of faculty and staff development, the president has set up a $150,000 "Risk Fund" for innovative projects. These funds are available to any member of the faculty, staff, or student body who can devise a new project with a demonstrated payback to the college. The college also offers to retrain any faculty or staff member displaced because of program cutbacks or elimination.

The College of DuPage prides itself in being a people-oriented institution, and reminds prospective students that the college is there for the large and small transitions in life, with the following invitation to all—"Come change with us."

President McAninch's leadership style can be summarized as quiet yet strong. "Hal keeps this place quiet and happy." "He maintains an even keel." There is however, ample evidence of solid, back-to-the-basics administration and excellent management. McAninch is also an active advocate of the college. When the state outlay process reached an impasse, his aggressive pursuit resulted in the authorization of two major buildings.

McAninch is extremely sensitive to the barriers facing college students. He believes in providing an accessible, low-cost, high-quality education and treating students as individual human beings. He sees his job as providing opportunities that will help students succeed and realize their full potential. He attempts to bring together diverse people with different strategies such that a critical mass is created which is "more than the sum of its parts."

George Mason University

Founded in 1957 as a two-year extension of the School of Arts and Sciences of the University of Virginia, George Mason University became an independent institution in 1972. In the past 13 years, this Fairfax, Virginia, institution's enrollment has grown from 3,000 to approximately 16,000, and the school has added over 40 master's and six Ph.D. degrees, acquired a 600-student law school, and established a second campus in Arlington, Virginia.

Fifteen miles from the nation's capital, George Mason is in the virtual center of one of America's most sophisticated, highly educated, and fastest growing suburban counties—Fairfax County, Virginia. Since 1960, the county's population has swollen from 150,000 to more than 650,000, and it has one of the nation's major concentrations of high technology industry—over 800 corporations employing around 100,000 people. This Northern Virginia region has one of the highest per capita income averages in the nation, an 80% college entrance rate for high school seniors, and claims over 40% of all Virginia Merit Scholars.

The university has, since its inception, been under continuous pressure from the regional community's constantly rising expectations.

As a consequence, George Mason has selected four specific development thrusts as its strategic plan: high quality undergraduate liberal arts education, a reflection of its beginning as an undergraduate liberal branch of the University of Virginia; policy studies, because of its location adjacent to the nation's capital; fine and performing arts, resulting from the university's desire to be a cultural focal point in an emerging community; and high technology, reflecting the region's primary business and industrial community.

However, most of the high technology development of George Mason has centered on the success of the nonprofit Institute for Science and Technology at George Mason, Inc. and a new, specialized School of Information Technology and Engineering created in 1984. To build a nationally recognized technology program, George Mason president George Johnson worked to develop an industry consensus on the importance of the university and the types of program the high tech community would support. He refers to this as being "industry-centered" as opposed to "university-centered." The results, in a four-year period, have been impressive.

The School of Information Technology and Engineering now has three departments, systems engineering, electrical engineering, and computer and information sciences: 1,300 undergraduates in three degree programs; 300 graduate students in six masters programs; the nation's first Ph.D. program in information technology; 38 full-time faculty with 25 new faculty lines appropriated for the fall of 1985; five endowed chairs; $2 million in research contracts; over $3 million in private support; and state appropriations for a 100,000 square foot research building.

In the performing arts, George Mason has moved more slowly in faculty recruiting but has aggressively developed facilities—a $17 million spectator facility and a $7 million performing arts instructional facility. A concert hall is in the planning stages.

When a member of our team asked a George Mason dean the

reasons for the university's dynamic development, he said, "Location, a growing student body that provides new money for new programs, and a president who can articulate a dream."

Kennesaw College

Founded in 1963 as a junior college, Kennesaw College is now a non-residential, coeducational senior college of the University System of Georgia. Kennesaw enjoys the reputation of being the fastest growing (and the seventh-largest) college in the 33-unit university system and offers academic programs in more than 20 fields. The degrees awarded by the college include 39 baccalaureate, 8 associate, and 2 master's degrees.

Kennesaw's potential for growth and excellence served as a major motivation for Betty L. Siegel to assume the presidency of the college in 1981. As a futurist, Siegel was struck with the potential Kennesaw College had to become a model contemporary college. The college is located north of Atlanta in Marietta, Georgia, an area experiencing unprecedented growth in population and economic development. Kennesaw is the only four-year state college between Cobb County, Georgia, and Chattanooga, Tennessee. The increased demand for higher education in the area is evidence in the 40% enrollment increase at Kennesaw from 1981-84. The fall 1984 enrollment was 5,800, and the 1985 enrollment is expected to top 6,500 students.

The average age of the Kennesaw student is 27 years, and two-thirds of the student body is employed full or part time. The college notes that if it were not for a popular two-year nursing program, virtually all students with declared majors would be enrolled in four-year programs, and that 6 of every 10 majors are in one of the business fields. Over the last five years, 98% of Kennesaw's teacher education graduates passed their state certification tests, the highest passing rate of all public and private teacher education programs in the state. In nursing, 95 to 100% of the program's graduates pass the state board examinations, and success rates for gaining entrance to professional schools are also very high.

Although Kennesaw's formal mission is one of education and service, its goal is excellence in all areas of the college. Kennesaw's teaching success is evident in the accomplishments of its students, but it was all made possible with careful planning and quality teaching faculty. Some notable characteristics of the 154 teaching faculty in 1983-84 include the following: 64% held terminal degrees, 36% were tenured, 46% were female, the average age was 41, 44% held the rank of associate or full professor, all but two with academic administrative responsibilities taught classes, the fulltime equivalent (FTE) student to teaching faculty ratio was 28 to 1, and the fall total student to teaching faculty ratio was 37 to 1. According to Siegel, the centrality of teaching is important at Kennesaw. It (teaching) has always been, and must continue to be the central task of the college. She believes in the strong need for faculty who believe that teaching is the facilitation of learning. She says "we must recruit talented, inviting, caring teachers and help them to create a nurturing, stimulating environment that exemplifies college-wide commitment to excellence in teaching... teachers who possess the most accurate understanding available about the learners who pass through their doors."

A variety of innovative student service programs are available at Kennesaw. In the area of counseling, advisement, and placement the college operates a center (CAPS), which incorporates the functions of personal and career counseling and job placement services and academic advisement. Specialized services are also available in the CAPS center, such as KC 101. KC 101 is an elective two-hour course available to freshmen who are interested in getting an orientation to Kennesaw College and to higher education in general.

The Center for Excellence in Teaching and Learning (CETL) at Kennesaw has been successful as an approach to learning and instructional effectiveness. The Center for Excellence in Teaching and Learning combines facilities for media services, learning laboratories, and a curriculum center in a joint venture between the college and local school systems to serve the instructional and professional needs of public school teachers. In addition, CETL has been placed as a department within the School of Education and, although it will continue to serve as a resource for media and curriculum development, it will also promote and sponsor programs, workshops, and seminars geared toward enhancing teaching effectiveness for faculty of all disciplines.

Kennesaw College is 1 of only 50 institutions in the nation with an endowed chair of private enterprise. The chair was made possible by contributions from financial institutions in the Atlanta area, and is considered to be a means of strengthening the college's academic programs and expanding the college's service and involvement in the community.

A new degree program in public and social services is the first of its kind in the state and one of the few in the entire country, and is designed to meet the needs and demands of business, government, and social service agencies. The program includes practical work experience, and development of interpersonal and interaction skills and flexibility, and graduates have career opportunities in federal and state government, private businesses, and community social service agencies.

When Betty Siegel arrived to assume the presidency, Kennesaw College was at a crossroads and "dead last in funding" among the 33 institutions in the Georgia system. Rather than remaining a school known as a way station, with students stopping in for a year or two before transferring to other colleges or universities, Kennesaw College decided to emphasize vitality and growth. Siegel notes that they could

> continue the posture that had served us well in a less demanding time or we could aspire to become a contemporary college in a contemporary setting for contemporary students . . . we can be what we're capable of becoming . . . we have the faculty, the staff and, we hope, the leadership that will enable us to do that. We have all the promise in the world. As someone who has been excited by what is happening here at Kennesaw College, I sincerely hope that this institution will never lose its dynamic qualities, its spirit of adventure, and its can-do attitude.

Lane Community College

Lane Community College, established in 1964, is a comprehensive public, two-year coeducational institution offering more than 50 technical/vocational programs, plus courses that can be applied toward degree programs at four-year colleges and universities.

Lane's 292-acre campus is located in Eugene, Western Oregon's leading industrial and marketing center, and has received awards for ease of access for the handicapped and for the quality and maintenance of its landscaping. The district served by the college covers 5,000 square miles, stretching from the Pacific Ocean to the Cascade Mountains, and in addition to its main campus Lane has three other teaching centers. The Downtown Center, housing the college's Business Assistance Center, adult education offices, and other community education programs, is located in the business district of Eugene. The Siuslaw Outreach Center in Florence serves residents of Western Lane County, and the Central Area Outreach Center in Cottage Grove serves the southern and eastern parts of the county. To serve students who cannot come to campus, Lane has a mobile classroom which visits outlying communities. Credit classes can also be taken via television in most of the communities in the college district.

Lane Community College enrolled 31,638 students during the 1983-84 academic year, with 12,672 in credit programs and 20,741 in noncredit community education. Most of the college's students come from the local district, and the average student age is 27 years, with 65% in the 21 to 50 age category. In 1983, Lane graduated 954 students with associate degrees or certificates, and 435 students graduated from the college's Adult High School Completion Program. Lane's nursing students had an impressive 98.6% pass rate on the 1983 Oregon licensing exam, higher than any other two- or four-year college in Oregon. A 1982 survey of Lane graduates found that 81% of the respondents were employed, with 82% of those working in jobs related to their studies at Lane.

From its inception, Lane has had a commitment to new and better ways to deliver education. The college has been willing to pioneer in new fields in order to better provide a wide range of educational opportunities meeting the diverse needs of their students, and has always given a high priority to exploring the uses of technology. Lane is an institution that seems to thrive on innovation and is one of only 18 community college districts in the nation invited to be a member of the League for Innovation in the Community College.

One of the most interesting initiatives recently undertaken at Lane is the Productivity Center. Established in 1981 to assist the college in creating an atmosphere for facilitating and enhancing change, the Productivity Center has two areas of focus: productivity improvement activities and institutional research and evaluation activities. The center provides the college's internal groups with opportunities to participate in decision making, implementation, and evaluation. These goals are achieved through such efforts as the implementation and coordination of "quality circles" and "verteams," the initiation of a productivity suggestion program, and establishment of a resource library on productivity practices.

Quality circles are a major activity at the center and consist of small groups of individuals working in the same area who voluntarily meet regularly with a facilitator to identify, analyze, and solve work-related problems. Using quality circle techniques to deal with problems identified by management, verteams are composed of a cross-section of college staff and exist only long enough to address specific concerns. During the Productivity Center's first three years, 15 quality circles involving approximately 160 participants were established, and some of the results of their activities include curriculum revisions, increased use of technology, procedural developments, and facility reorganization.

The Business Assistance Center was created in 1982 to meet the needs of local business and to bolster the county's economic development. Attempting to meet the needs of both urban and rural constituents, the center offers short-term, practical educational opportunities to area businesses. During the center's first year of operation, 31 classes, seminars, and workshops enrolled approximately 2,000 individuals. The center also provides technical assistance to small business operators and potential entrepreneurs, and during 1982-83 more than 500 people were given direct technical assistance by the center's staff. The Business Assistance Center was selected by the state of Oregon as a model educational program, and efforts are underway to establish similar centers at other community colleges in the state.

There are a number of innovations indicative of Lane's attempts to "find better ways of doing things," such as permitting designated departments the use of a VISA card for purchasing inexpensive items, a payroll direct deposit option, major efforts in managing and conserving energy, and a staff development office (with a full-time director) that helps in the development of programs like computer literacy for staff, use of industry for teacher training, a technology master plan, and programs to reduce staff burnout and increase management effectiveness.

Under the leadership of the late Eldon Schafer, Lane Community College received national attention, not only for instructional innovation but also for its administrative cost saving. President Schafer noted that colleges and universities must "increase productivity in the 80's if you want to be around in the 90's."

Schafer defined the seven operational elements of productivity that formed the foundation of Lane's Carnegie Corporation grant which established the National Community College Productivity Center: first, increase the learning of students; second, help staff become more efficient; third, make the community college accessible to a wider range of students; fourth, lower the cost of producing a unit of education; fifth, reduce tuition rates; sixth, develop and implement a more efficient administrative organization; and seventh, manage facilities and resources more effectively.

Asked to comment on Schafer's contributions to Lane Community College, Dale Parrell, formerly president of Lane and now president of the American Association of Community and Junior Colleges, described Schafer in the 1984 fall issue of the Lane Community College report as something of an institution himself. He asserts that Schafer gained wide recognition as the leader of a school that is, in turn, "a leader and pacesetter among the community colleges of the nation."

Maricopa Community Colleges

The seven two-year colleges that make up this community college district serve one of the nation's fastest growing urban/suburban communities—Maricopa County, Phoenix, Arizona. One of the most desirable Sunbelt locations benefiting from a state-encouraged high technology industry concentration, Maricopa County has almost two million people. The county planners project a 40% growth by 1995.

Maricopa Community College District (MCCD) is unique in

several respects. First, it is not just one large community college (like Northern Virginia and DuPage, in this study, or Miami Dade, the nation's largest). It is a system of seven individual institutions, each with distinct service missions and its own president.

Maricopa Community College District is organizationally comparable, to the Dallas, Los Angeles, and Chicago community college districts. It is the third largest such community college organization in the country. But the Maricopa Community College is unique. It is 23 years old yet is just now emerging as a major national community college force—perhaps a prototypical institution. This emergence in the 1980s is due to three factors: the explosive growth of the Phoenix area; a strategic vision of a community college developing to meet the educational needs of a rapidly developing American metropolitan area; and a leader who brought a unique set of experiences and vision to the college, Paul Elsner.

Under Elsner's leadership, the Maricopa Community Colleges have several thrusts, including a 10-year, $150-million capital improvement program for buildings and equipment.

Maricopa Community College District serves a significant minority population and has undertaken a number of unique initiatives. For example, in 1984 one of the institutions, South Mountain College, received a three-year, $225,000 Ford Foundation grant to assist minority and low-income students in their transition from the community college to a university. This is one of five such programs funded by the Ford Foundation in the country. In 1983, 20 of the college's students transferred to Arizona State University, Northern Arizona University, and Grand Canyon College.

To meet the requirements of its technology-based business, MCCD has taken several steps. The first is a high technology industries advisory council to help the colleges understand and meet the needs of this unique and emerging business community. Second, MCCD has made a multi-million dollar commitment to computerize the colleges. A mainframe-dominated approach to computing was abandoned in favor of a decentralized system which is based on a comprehensive network of mini and microcomputers. Two thousand instruments are now on the network with key administrators, faculty, and board members having access to an electronic mail system via microcomputers in their homes. The chancellor, who conceived this undertaking, remains committed to every faculty member having a personal computer and computer literacy is being achieved.

While the MCCD is large (65,000 credit students and 55,000 noncredit students) and progressive, it is taking nothing for granted. To focus on the future, a Joint Council on Educational Priorities (JCEP) is convened periodically to respond to Elsner's "Chancellor's Blueprint for Educational Planning." The Joint Council on Educational Priorities suggested a set of 10 priorities in 1982: articulation; computer literacy; developmental education; general education and transfer education; honors programs; occupational education; staff development; student assessment, advisement, and tracking; student recruitment and marketing; and student services. The Joint Council presented a rationale, description, and recommendations for each of these priorities.

Finally, this college district has distinguished itself because of the attention given to that most important resource, the faculty and staff. The district offers its employees flexible benefits and early retirements, a well-organized physical fitness program, a guarantee of no layoffs via a comprehensive retraining program, grants for professional development, and such services as financial and psychological counseling.

Paul Elsner demonstrates two unique leadership characteristics. First, the chancellor places immense importance on people. He goes to great lengths to find talented people for his staff. His managerial style has a distinct human relations orientation. Additionally, his working relationships are superb with direct contact and a personal touch quite evident.

Second, Dr. Elsner is a futurist. He possesses a unique vision which suggests he is ahead of his times. His creativity and ingenuity result in a spectrum of new ideas, which is continually being presented to his staff.

Paul Elsner believes that organizations must pay close attention to their external environment and accommodate the rapid changes that will be needed. He asserts "the job of a leader is to manage orderly change processes."

Marylhurst College for Lifelong Learning

Marylhurst College for Lifelong Learning is now in its eleventh year as a nontraditional coeducational college for traditional and nontraditional students. Prior to its reorganization in 1974, it had been a Catholic women's college operated by the Sisters of the Holy Names. When it was established in 1859 in Portland, Oregon, as St. Mary's Academy, it was the first women's college in the state. In 1974, as the Marylhurst College for Lifelong Learning, it became the first liberal arts college in the northwest devoted to the educational needs of the working adult.

The college has been at its present location south of Lake Oswego since 1930. Marylhurst is bounded on one side by the west bank of the Willamette River and is surrounded by thick banks of Douglas fir. On a clear day, Mount Hood, as the natives say "comes out" with astonishing clarity.

Marylhurst literally died to become what its officers claim was the first accredited degree-granting institution in the nation devoted primarily to lifelong learning and granting college credit for experiential learning. By 1974 dwindling enrollments and rising costs had swamped the college's books in a sea of red ink and Marylhurst closed its doors.

In death, however, Marylhurst was more like a phoenix than a suicide, for the day after its closing it rose from its own ashes—reopening as the Marylhurst Education Center, a "College for Lifelong Learning" with a strong emphasis on experiential learning.

Marylhurst grew rapidly after its reorganization in 1974, and as enrollment grew the college became financially stable. Over $500,000 from the Kellogg Foundation supported program development. In 1983-84, the Collins Foundation created a $200,000 Stabilization Fund, and a $330,000 model Management Information System project funded by the M.J. Murdock Charitable Trust improved the college's cost effectiveness. Financial aid resources have grown with a $50,000 Hearst Foundation endowed scholarship and a $30,000 endowed scholarship in honor of Sister Veronica Baxter, president of the college from 1974-84.

The average age of the Marylhurst student is 39, but ages range from 17-70; last year the college graduated an 85-year-old student.

Since most students at Marylhurst work full time, the college schedules numerous evening and weekend classes, in addition to providing them with the opportunity to earn up to 90 quarter hours of college credits for work and life experiences in a Prior Learning Experience (PLE) Program. Degrees offered include: bachelor of arts degrees with majors in art, crafts, music, and pastoral ministries; bachelor of fine arts; bachelor of music; bachelor of science in management; as well as individualized bachelor of arts degrees with majors in communication, humanities, human studies, social science, science/math, and interdisciplinary studies. In addition, a master of science is offered in management and a master of arts in art therapy. Marylhurst enrolled approximately 2,000 students in the 1983-84 academic year, 85% of whom attended part time. About half of the 450 full-time equivalent enrollment students were in degree-granting programs, and many students continue to take classes for individual or career enrichment after receiving degrees. President Nancy Wilgenbusch views the concept of adult education as a "mission" rather than a profession. She explained in a recent interview: "It's a fundamental question of freedom . . . without education, people have no alternatives, no choices—no freedom."

Marylhurst attempts to provide:

> a different way to learn and an environment in which education is more than just textbook learning . . . Marylhurst faculty add an important dimension to this new approach to education, since classroom teaching is based on their experience in the business or professional world, or in other settings. In a sense our instructors practice what they teach.

President Wilgenbusch, who is most impressed with the Marylhurst faculty calls them "the most committed group" she has ever worked with. She claims she has to worry about them working too *hard*, not too little.

In addition to the Prior Learning Experience Program, Marylhurst has created a Division of Individualized Studies, a program linking classic liberal arts education to the needs and interests of the adult learner. The college states that the division has a "frankly activist perspective, which assumes that Marylhurst learners are interested in using their education today to better their own lives, as well as the lives of those around them, in their families, organizations, and society in general." Three themes guide the division's curriculum: activism, contemporary values orientation, and traditional theory. Corresponding with these perspectives, the learner is asked to address the values orientation by completing a Life Seminar (Living Issues for the Eighties); the traditions and theory component by completing a "perspectives" course; and the activist dimension by completing an internship designed to explore the challenge of being an effective agent for change.

Marylhurst also has a new major in human studies, which integrates personal and professional development, experiential and classroom learning, generalist and specialist studies, prior and current learning, and process and content. Designed for the returning adult interested in "helping activities," the human studies program has received national attention as a model innovation in adult education. This B.A. program is composed of two parts. First, the Human Studies Foundations colloquia consist of five courses that help the student "develop a comprehensive view of what it is to be human and how quality may be introduced or enhanced in everyday experience." Second, the Specific Problem studies develop the ability to actualize "a comprehensive philosophy of quality" by acquiring expertise concerning at least one specific human problem or issue, such as domestic violence, substance abuse, organizational training, or environmental advocacy.

Asked to explain what makes Marylhurst unique, Wilgenbusch cites "smaller classes, individually tailored education, an outstanding advisory system, and services for midlife career changes." She adds that "I like to think we provide hassle-free education. There are no long lines; we get the person in to see whomever he or she needs very quickly. Adults are demanding; they know what they want, and they won't be spoon fed."

Sister Veronica Baxter, president of Marylhurst from 1974-84, stated that "our society is experiencing a knowledge boom, but a wisdom vacuum. Lifelong learning is the key to wisdom. In such a society, claims Baxter, Marylhurst is unique. She says that "In an age when computers speak to computers, Marylhurst voices the human dimension. Adults seek meaning, fulfillment, change, dialogue among equals—Marylhurst *is* that resource."

Northeast Missouri State University

Founded in 1867, Northeast Missouri State University (NEMSU) was the first regional state university in Missouri and one of the first institutions of higher education west of the Mississippi River. The university is located on 140 acres in Kirksville, Missouri, and offers 140 four-year programs, 21 one-and two-year certificate programs, and 25 graduate majors in 13 academic divisions. The enrollment at Northeast Missouri State is approximately 7,000 students, of which 72% receive some type of financial aid or scholarship. The student/teacher ratio is about 19:1, and 60% of the faculty hold doctorates.

The traditional mission of Northeast Missouri State University was teacher preparation, but in the early 1970s, under the leadership of President Charles J. McClain, the institution began to move away from being primarily a teacher education school. In 1971, a commission was appointed by the school's board of regents to chart a new course for NEMSU, and in 1973 seven institutional goals that outlined the basic purposes of the school were presented by the commission. The goals were primarily output oriented, with two tasks related to the internal operations of the university. However, this was only the beginning of a long process of mission definition for Northeast Missouri State. In 1977, President McClain posed a number of questions to the university community that resulted in the further refinement of the mission. Finally, in 1984, a draft of the statement of purpose was presented: "The mission of the university is to achieve excellence through (1) a liberal arts-based higher education; (2) nationally competitive preprofessional, professional, and career oriented programs; (3) selected graduate programs at the master and specialist levels in areas that have achieved excellence at the undergraduate level; (4) pure and applied research efforts consistent with the teaching and public service functions of the university; (5) continuing education opportunities which meet national needs and are a natural outgrowth of existing programs, and (6) public service."

In addition, Northeast Missouri has made a commitment to providing a quality education for its students in both the cognitive and affective domains. The university's objectives are for students to (1) gain substantive knowledge in the liberal arts through a strong general education; (2) acquire extensive knowledge in their major fields of study and be nationally competitive in their majors at the time of graduation; (3) further develop analytical, speaking, writing, and decision-making/problem-solving skills; (4) develop an interest in and skills for independent, life-long learning; (5) increase cultural appreciation and awareness; and (6) improve their self-image, confidence, persistence, and social and leadership skills.

The American Association of State Colleges and Universities named Northeast Missouri State University a co-recipient of the 1983 G. Theodore Mitau Award, for "Innovation and Excellence in State Colleges and Universities," for its Value-Added Learning Program. This comprehensive and systematic value-added model of assessment had its beginnings in 1973 and now "sets the tone for the entire university," notes President McClain.

The Value-Added Program at NEMSU was initiated to improve the quality of undergraduate education through course and academic evaluations using results from standardized tests. These evaluations are accomplished by measuring "the knowledge students bring to Northeast as freshmen and the additional knowledge—the value added—at the end of their sophomore and senior years." In addition, attitudinal surveys of freshmen are administered during orientation, there is a yearly Institutional Student Survey, and a Graduate Student Questionnaire, and alumni and their employers are surveyed to further assess the impact of an NEMSU education. Evaluation results are used to pinpoint weak areas in the curriculum, and the program has had a large impact on the university. Curriculum changes have been made, faculty and students alike have great praise for the program, and the results are impressive. For example, in 1982, the 12 Northeast Missouri accounting students who took the certified public accountant licensing test had a higher average score than the students from any other institution of higher learning in America.

As President McClain notes, "Through the use of this value-added system of assessment, the university aims to maximize its human and technological resources for the education of its students. It aims to be sure it is providing quality education that assures its students of competency in the marketplace upon graduation." The president also believes that "the public wants assurance today that a college degree has some integrity."

McClain, himself, was the key factor in the university's success in implementing the value-added approach. His quiet persistence is extraordinary and, perhaps, the most important long-term factor in the school's success. For example, for over a decade, McClain has personally interviewed every serious candidate for a faculty position, carefully explaining his vision for the university and the value-added program. He wanted to build a faculty committed to quantifiable teaching and learning, and he has been successful.

There is broad support and admiration at NEMSU for what McClain has accomplished. One veteran staff member told us "It's clear that a president makes a difference in what can be achieved in higher education. It's easy to draw comparisons to the other institutions in the state where leader after leader was able to achieve little distinction, happy to dwell on the tired themes of not enough money and another conference championship."

McClain put the institution's resources into the instructional program. People are continually surprised that NEMSU, with 7,000 students, has only one vice president, three deans, and a half-dozen directors—a virtually flat and certainly spartan administrative structure.

Northern Arizona University

Northern Arizona University (NAU) is one of three public universities in Arizona, all with one board of control—the Arizona Board of Regents. Northern Arizona University was originally organized as the state's normal school for teacher training, but it has, over the years, become a comprehensive university.

The university has a unique location in Flagstaff: at an elevation of 7,000 feet, the 689-acre campus at the base of the San Francisco peaks is situated amid a landscape that reminds one more of alpine Colorado than Arizona. Founded in 1899, NAU has grown to 12,500 students and is in the process of carving out a state-wide role for itself.

Within the state, the university's reputation is growing dramatically, and national recognition is also increasing, in part because of a strategic plan frequently referred to as "excellence one college at a time." This plan has been emerging over the past several years under the guidance of the university's president, Gene Hughes.

The strategic plan of Northern Arizona University has several focuses, one of which is the reorganization and reinvigoration of education, the creative arts, and communications, and units like the design and technology college. Efforts to significantly raise the effectiveness, excellence, and, ultimately, recognition of these units, involved a systematic, grass-roots approach with a great deal of faculty involvement. These efforts seem to be a model for consensus thinking and planning.

The NAU plan for achieving excellence specifically emphasizes three (or perhaps more) programmatic areas: education, forestry, and hotel and restaurant management. In these cases, the involvement with change is not nearly so general: the goal is building a locally (in the state) and perhaps nationally distinctive program.

The School of Forestry is the only program in the southwest accredited by the Society of American Foresters, and is distinctive for several reasons: (1) it has three semesters of "wholly integrated" forestry instruction when the student takes no other classes; (2) the university is situated in the middle of the nation's oldest experimental forest and the largest ponderosa pine forest in America; and (3) Northern Arizona University's forestry program has gained substantial recognition from the U.S. Forest Service and foresters across America.

While NAU is naturally appropriate for a high quality program in forestry, the same cannot be said of its drive for excellence in teacher education. Even though it was Arizona's only normal school (originally devoted exclusively to teacher training), the university's location far from the state's population centers would seem to be an insurmountable barrier to becoming the dominant university in the state in this discipline.

However, shrewd planning, determination to use the university for public good, and institutional flexibility, among other factors, allowed NAU to take on a leadership role in reforming teacher education in Arizona and a definitive state-wide mission in education roughly equivalent to that awarded Arizona State University in engineering. As previously discussed, President Hughes developed the idea to create a state center for excellence in education with a state-wide mission, and sold it to everyone from the governor to the state school superintendent, the Board of Regents, and the legislature.

This center will provide training for students entering the education profession as teachers, administrators, or counselors; provide in-service training for teachers and administrators who already are in the state's education system; focus on greater unification of pedagogy and subject matter; coordinate teacher internships in the public schools; work directly in the public schools, utilizing newly created methods and materials to improve student performance in basic subjects; choose master teachers from the public schools who will hold joint appointments with the center and their school district and in the summer will teach and study on the university campus; focus research on practical classroom effectiveness, rather than esoterica; and look for solutions to problems in the public schools and the transmission of new knowledge in the classroom.

Northern Arizona is turning its attention to a new school of hotel and restaurant management. There is a sense of excitement at NAU, and the faculty have a growing sense of pride and commitment. For the first time, they feel just as important to Arizona as the University of Arizona.

Northern Virginia Community College

Located in the metropolitan Washington, D.C., area, Northern Virginia Community College (NVCC) is one of 23 state-supported two-year colleges in the Virginia Community College System, which was established in 1966 to ensure that individuals in the state are provided a "continuing, low cost opportunity for the development and extension of their skills and knowledge." Northern

Virginia Community College is a multi-campus comprehensive two-year institution emphasizing occupational/technical programs.

Established in 1964 as Northern Virginia Technical College, the college held its first classes in 1965 in a renovated warehouse, with an initial enrollment of 765 students and 46 faculty and staff members. In 1966, the name of the college was changed to Northern Virginia Community College when the state's community college system was established. At that time the college's program become more comprehensive, with the addition of college transfer curricula to the traditional occupational/technical programs, and during the next three years approximately 400 acres were purchased in the Northern Virigina area to provide the sites for five permanent campuses of the community college. By 1975, the fifth campus had moved into its permanent buildings, and the college began offering courses through the sixth branch of the institution, the Extended Learning Institute.

Northern Virginia Community College offers two-year degrees and one-year certificates, and offers programs in occupational technical education, college transfer, general education, continuing education, community service, special training, developmental studies, and cooperative education. Over 88% of the curricula at NVCC are occupational/technical programs. In 1984, 65% of NVCC graduates received occupational or technical degrees or certificates, and 35% received college transfer degrees.

Northern Virginia Community College is the largest institution of higher education in Virginia and the second largest credit enrollment multi-campus community college in the United States. The phenomenal growth of NVCC has occurred during the tenure of Richard J. Ernst, who assumed the presidency just three years after the college opened. Together, the five campuses enrolled a total of 35,067 students in the fall of 1983, and during the 1983-84 fiscal year 59,322 individuals were enrolled in credit courses, 16,412 in noncredit continuing education, 37,740 in community services, and 63,568 in student services. The average student age is 28 years, with over 63% of the student body between the age of 22 and 45. Most of the students are from the Northern Virginia area, and 22% attend on a full-time basis. Northern Virginia Community employs approximately 500 full-time and 850 part-time faculty members.

One of the most successful initiatives undertaken at NVCC has been the ELI, an independent study program that enables students to pursue college work without attending classes. The ELI offers over 40 credit courses in business, science, and the humanities. Students may register at any time and are allowed up to six months to complete most courses. Course material is available to students through textbooks and printed material, audio/visual cassettes, television and radio programs, and teleconferencing, which enables one instructor to lecture to classes at many locations. During the first 18 months of operation after its founding in 1975, the ELI enrolled more than 4,500 students. Other flexible programs offered at NVCC are Weekend College, in-community classes, self-paced study, accelerated summer schedules, and customized training for business and industry in which the college works with local companies in special training programs.

Northern Virginia Community College has recently implemented a marketing plan designed to "facilitate the identification of present and future needs of NVCC's public." The marketing plan was conceived in response to a question directed to the college community by President Ernst in 1983: "How do we as a college community respond to the challenge of maximizing the effective use of shrinking resources in order to continue providing leadership in meeting the ever-changing educational needs of those whom we serve?" As Ernst noted, "The question in itself is neither mysterious nor profound. . . . It represents, however, the challenge of the 1980s. . . ." Northern Virginia Community College's plan consists of four areas of emphasis: product development and improvement, enrollment, research, and communications (PERC). The objectives of the "product" category are to evaluate and enhance the quality of NVCC products and their relation to current and future market needs, respond to the specialized education and training needs of industry, and identify and develop alternative resources consistent with that of the college mission. "Enrollment" involves meeting enrollment projections and encouraging students to complete their educational objectives. "Research" objectives are to establish a computerized information system to support college marketing efforts and enhance decision-making processes, increase knowledge about prospective students and clients, and identify market competition for each college program. The objectives of the "communication" category are to project a positive image of NVCC, enhance the college's communication system to support marketing efforts, and encourage, stimulate, and support marketing at all levels of the college. (In a miscellaneous, or other, category, NVCC goals are to identify and provide necessary resources for attainment of marketing objectives, to integrate the marketing process into the college's educational master planning process, and facilitate the marketing plan and the further development of marketing strategies for the college.)

Northern Virginia Community College's marketing plan is a strategic plan designed to ensure that NVCC responds to the challenges of the 1980s. "NVCC's future is interrelated with its ability to measure the needs, interests, and demands of the consuming and supporting public and the ability of its personnel to deliver what is needed . . . NVCC has taken the first steps toward a secure, growth oriented future."

Interestingly, NVCC's phenomenal growth from some 2,000 students in 1968 when Ernst took over as president to the 35,000 plus students in credit courses (not counting thousands of others in noncredit courses) in 1984 came about largely because the college is the only community college serving a growing population of some 1.2 million people. It seemed in NVCC's early years that it had to only open the doors, start a new program, or offer a night class in an area high school to have practically every seat filled.

So the initial challenge was not to market the college, but to put the infrastructure in place to accommodate the large and ever increasing number of students. This is where Ernst excelled. His organizational abilities are broadly recognized both within and outside the college. We asked Dick Ernst to give us some of his thinking on educational leadership. The following four items give one a sense of his approach.

1. An effective leader must search continuously for new ideas and innovative approaches for doing things better—for improving any area of the institution.

2. Fundamental to a leader's success is a willingness to surround himself/herself with people who have more expertise than

he/she has in any given area of responsibility. Creative, competent people are the key to success in any organization. The leader must also be willing to delegate in order to capitalize upon this expertise.

3. Committed people, working together to fulfill a clearly articulated mission make the difference between institutions.

4. There must be a willingness to search for new ideas, consider change and innovation where appropriate, and capitalize upon opportunities that present themselves.

Queens College

Queens College is a private, church-related undergraduate liberal arts college for women located in Charlotte, North Carolina. It was founded in 1857 as the Charlotte Female Institute, renamed the Seminary for Girls in 1881, and became known as the Presbyterian College for Women after affiliating with the Presbyterian Synod of North Carolina in 1886. In 1912 the college came to be known by its present name.

In 1912 Queens College moved to its present location, the Myers Park area of Charlotte, in Southeastern Mecklenburg County. The idyllic campus is located in an affluent, highly educated, and heavily populated section of Charlotte. Known as the southeast's banking and distribution center, Charlotte serves as corporate headquarters for two of the nation's 100 largest banks, and Charlotte's total banking assets of more than $35 billion are more than any other city between Philadelphia and Dallas. Of Fortune 500 companies, 308 have operations in Charlotte. Many people are surprised to learn that within a 100-mile radius, Charlotte has a larger population than Atlanta.

In spite of its obvious geographic advantages, Queens was floundering in February 1978, when Billy Wireman assumed the presidency. Enrollment had steadily declined to around 500, almost 20% of the faculty had been released in retrenchment efforts, and there was a critical budget deficit. It seemed likely that Queens would merge or close. Today, however, the student body numbers over 1,200, there is an operating surplus for the first time in 17 years, and the endowment has increased. Most of the faculty attribute the change of events at Queens to President Wireman, whom they described as tireless, dynamic, and visionary. His ability to combine strategic planning with marketing has turned Queens around. Wireman's short-term goal in the recovery process was to address enrollment and financial problems, and his long-term goal was to build a sound future. The four main points of the Wireman's strategic plan were to: (1) enhance the existing programs; (2) create new academic programs for an adult and nontraditional clientele; (3) provide strong financial management; and (4) initiate a fund-raising effort based on the success of the other goals.

Fund raising was crucial to the process. Wireman was convinced that the key to prosperity was not dwelling on "How can we survive?" but asking "How can we serve?" A national publication said "The way Queens College administrators talk about 'service,' one might imagine they wear the word emblazoned on sweatshirts. The enthusiasm is well warranted. The school's commitment to serving the needs of local business people has fostered a creative restructuring of academics—which in turn has led to rising enrollment and new financial support." Wireman insisted that the service had to precede the financial support. He said, "You've got to be seen as an investment and not a charity."

Considerable national attention in higher education has been focused on Wireman for his ability to recast an institution's identity. One of Wireman's first orders of business upon coming to Queens was asking the faculty to justify the school's existence by determining "the emerging educational needs of the community that Queens can help meet in ways that are compatible with our available resources and our traditional values." The needs determined by this process served as the basis for the four-point strategic plan.

A faculty member who remembers Wireman's early days at Queens states:

> Billy is a true leader. He said we could cut expenses, and fail or survive, or spend, and fail or survive. He emphasized the positive so strongly that he had us wanting to borrow and spend—make it pretty here again, hire new faculty, add new programs, fix the library. We

were happy that we were going to expand rather than reduce our offerings and chance becoming more, rather than assuredly becoming less.
At least with Billy as president, we knew if we were going to go, we'd
go in a blaze of glory.

Asked to comment on his perspective on leadership, Wireman
draws an important distinction between management and leadership. He defines management as "getting things done through
others and basically assuring that things are done right." While he
recognizes the importance of this function, he adds that it "often
does not get at the conceptual issues of vision, purpose, and direction." He explains that leadership means "having a vision which not
only sees that things are done right, but more importantly, ensures
that the institution is doing the right things." Wireman has always
taken the position that

> leaders ought to be active, galvanizing influences in helping institu-
> tions develop a philosophic clarity and precision, a vision, a sense of
> significance, excitement and momentum—all undergirded with a
> moral commitment which helps individuals transcend the immediacy
> of the moment and become a part in creating a just, enlightened, and
> humane society.

Wireman further believes that "competency in management can
be purchased and evaluated by competent leaders, but to have a
place well managed is not enough. The leadership role is critical
because without it, there would never be any questioning of the
goals and purposes of the institution, but rather just a constant assessment of how we can do better the things we are doing now." He
adds that "leaders, in short, ought to lead. If all we do is manage,
then there will develop a great collective vacuum begging to be
filled with some sense of vision, relevancy, and moral purpose."

The faculty member who labeled Wireman a true leader added
that "Billy's sense of vision has given all of us a sense of relevance."

Wireman, in short, appears to be, in his own terms, "a leader
who is leading."

Since Wireman's arrival in 1978, Queens has:

- Increased total enrollment by 128% from 541 degree students
  to 1,236 in the fall of 1985

- Increased enrollment in the College of Arts and Sciences—the traditional undergraduate college for Women only—by 34% from 489 to 653, with a 52% increase in the number of resident students
- Added new undergraduate majors in nursing, accounting, computer science, and communications
- Established the New Dimensions Program for women aged 23 or older who are returning to college
- Started New College at Queens, a coed baccalaureate program for working adults whose classes meet at night and on Saturday, which now enrolls 402 men and women
- Started the Graduate School at Queens which offers masters in business administration and masters in education degrees and beginning fall 1985 in Liberal Arts
- Raised academic standards across the board—the SAT scores of entering freshman have risen over 70 points, and the GMAT scores of the MBA students place them in the top quartile nationally
- Established privately funded merit scholarship programs in each academic division to attract outstanding students—Presidential Scholarships in the College of Arts and Sciences, Ginter Fellowships in New College, and Blumenthal Fellowships in the Graduate School
- Established the Queens Institute of Lifelong Learning (QUILL), which is the noncredit arm of the college (this year 7,000–8,000 area residents will take one of the courses, workshops, or seminars offered by QUILL)
- Systematically reduced operating deficits—in 1977 Queens finished the year with a $600,000 operating deficit, but since 1982 the college has operated in the black, and in 1984 achieved its first operating surplus in 17 years and had another operating surplus in fiscal 1985
- Greatly increased asset income—assets that earned the college less than $200,000 in 1977 now provide over $600,000 a year in income
- Successfully completed two major fund-raising campaigns

securing $6.1 million in contributions against combined goals of $5.5 million

- Reduced bank debt from $1.9 million in 1978 to a current balance of $435,000, while also adding over $2 million in new endowment

- Established Queens Compute, a personal computer training center serving both the general public and the corporate community

Despite the addition of New College and the Graduate School as coeducational degree granting units, the liberal arts women's college known as the College of Arts and Sciences remains central to the institution. Project Renaissance, the development of an academic plan to "build the College of Arts and Sciences into one of the most future-oriented and distinctive undergraduate church-related colleges for women in the country," is now underway at Queens. Its foundation is liberal arts and career preparation in combination, and its purpose is "to produce graduates with a solid foundation of liberal arts study, emphasizing interconnected thinking and in-depth study in a major discipline, who will also have the necessary experience—built out of a four-year program which relates theory and practice—to achieve success in graduate school, professional school, and the world of work."

Along with Project Renaissance, another project for Queens's future is in progress. That is Queens '90, a seven-year academic and financial development plan for acquiring a minimum of $15,510,000 in annual and capital gifts over the period of 1983-90. Billy Wireman is confident that Queens '90 will succeed "because Queens is now regarded as a valuable asset to our community, state, and region." Nobody appears to disagree.

Rensselaer Polytechnic Institute

Rensselaer Polytechnic Institute (RPI) is located in Troy, New York, in the Hudson River Valley area. Founded in 1824, RPI is one of the country's oldest science and engineering institutions, and is a private coeducational school with a total enrollment of approximately 6,500 students, of which 4,500 are undergraduates. Of the freshman class, 60% receive some kind of financial aid. Admission to RPI is competitive—85% of the students enrolled graduated from high school in the top fifth of their class, and there were about 6,400 applicants for 1,200 spaces in 1984.

Prior to 1970, RPI was primarily an undergraduate engineering school and depended extensively on tuition for support. Caught in a financial squeeze in the early 1970s, the school experienced problems with operating costs and low faculty salaries. When George Low assumed the presidency at RPI in 1976, the institution was ready for a new direction. President Low garnered the support of the entire college community in preparing a long-range plan for development, which was called Rensselaer 2000 and consisted of a clear statement of institutional goals and objectives for RPI.

Rensselaer Polytechnic Institute flourished with George Low as president. Research support has grown from less than $5 million in 1976 to more than $22 million. The quality of admitted freshmen has increased, and the graduate school has been expanded. In addition, RPI has been successful in focusing its energy and resources on major initiatives in science and engineering. For example, RPI has been involved in space-related research for more than two decades (RPI students and faculty built a Mars Rover for NASA in 1965). Also, in 1982, the Army awarded RPI $3.1 million over a four-year period to establish one of three national centers for research in rotary wing (helicopter), technology.

The Center for Industrial Innovation (CII) is a major initiative underway at RPI and is considered "crucial for the revitalization of industry" in the state of New York because of its potential for "becoming a model for university-corporate cooperation." The $30 million center is presently under construction on the RPI campus and is scheduled for completion in 1986. The CII will house three major research centers already functioning at the institution: the Center for Integrated Electronics, the Center for Manufacturing Productivity and Technology Transfer, and the Center for Interactive Computer Graphics. The Center for Integrated Electronics has approximately 25 ongoing research projects, and since its foundation in 1981 has received major funding from such sources as the Pew Memorial Trust, IBM, Timex, Digital Equipment, and General

Electric. The Center for Manufacturing Productivity and Technology Transfer was established in 1979 and is working on approximately 30 projects aimed at increasing American industrial productivity, such as research into the application of robotics in composites manufacturing. Finally, the Center for Interactive Computer Graphics houses about 35 research projects in geometric modeling, graphics algorithms, data exchange, and finite element analysis.

In addition to the Center for Industrial Innovation, RPI established an "incubator" program, which assists in the start-up of entrepreneurial enterprises. Through the development of Rensselaer Industrial Park, the institution encourages new ideas and enterprise, and "the outcome for the companies and for the university is a mutually supportive environment."

Rensselaer Polytechnic Institute has become a model for effective industry and university partnerships. In 1983 George Low explained his overriding principle concerning the relationship between university and industry: "University-industry linkages will be successful only if they are based on educational programs of intrinsic academic value." Low stated that an institution must develop educational goals and plans, and carry them out with distinction. Rensselaer Polytechnic Institute has been a first-rate success in this endeavor.

At the time George Low, an RPI alumnus, became president of the institution in 1976, the institution was in trouble. However, Low found in the person of George Ansel, the engineering dean, an ally with his own vision of RPI's future. Together, Low mostly outside and Ansel mostly working inside, they forged a new dynamic in Troy.

Low was good at selling big ideas to government and industry leaders. After all, he was substantially responsible for persuading President Kennedy to support the man on the moon program. He repeated that performance in Troy by getting the governor of New York, leading industrialists, and major government agencies to invest in the future of America's oldest engineering school. He also knew how to orchestrate an organization with many bright and complex people toward a common goal.

Finally, the late George Low appeared to be in a hurry to get RPI back on track and, once again, a national force in engineering education. Not only did Low keep the institution focused on the long-range vision, he also worked feverishly toward that goal.

Rensselaer Polytechnic Institute's genes were changes by Low's vision and approach, and today his spirit still drives it.

St. Norbert College

St. Norbert College is a private Catholic school for men and women located in De Pere, Wisconsin. St. Norbert describes itself as a Christian community of learners that attempts to "perfect the personal, moral, and intellectual development of each student" in a liberal arts tradition. This basic philosophy has not changed since the founding of the college by the Norbertine Fathers in 1898, although the mission of the school has been refined over the years.

St. Norbert is today a very different school than it was in the late 1960s and early 1970s, during which time the college experienced severe enrollment and financial problems and deteriorating academic standards. Under the leadership of President Neil Webb, the college made a remarkable recovery: the budget was consistently balanced, the endowment fund grew at an exponential rate, and enrollment and retention rates increased dramatically.

The resurgence of St. Norbert can, in part, be attributed to the college having regained a clear sense of identity and mission. The first moves Webb made as president were to "get people thinking positively about the school" and to enlist the constituent groups of the St. Norbert community (students, faculty, trustees, administrators, parents, and alumni) in formulating a consensual statement of goals for the college. The statement of goals and objectives that emerged is twofold and clearly explained in the college catalogue.

First, the college committed itself to the personal, moral, and intellectual development of its students. The college strives for this by (1) emphasizing activities that help students develop personal goals, a sense of self-worth and self-understanding, and open, honest, and trusting relationships with others; (2) encouraging students to clarify their own values and beliefs; and (3) making students self-educating people. Second, St. Norbert "committed itself to maintaining an environment in which such developmental changes can take place and will be fostered," through open communication among its members, efficient operation, and quality academic programs.

Finally, the St. Norbert experience is an emphasis on a "total package of quality," and it is this commitment to quality that has brought the college to its present state of vitality and growth. In fact, the consensual statement of goals that emerged in the mid-1970s is today described as a single concept, quality, and St. Norbert has developed its institutional priorities with this concept in mind.

The first priority in achieving the goal of quality was to make St. Norbert a more selective institution. President Webb decided to limit enrollment and raise the admission standards. Enrollment at first suffered a drastic decline but eventually began to rise, and the 1982-83 figures stabilized at 1,720 (an increase of 245 over the 1972-73 enrollment). The 1982-83 statistics also indicate that applications for admissions had almost doubled (1,368 in 1982-83), as did the number of admitted freshmen who placed in the upper one-fifth of their classes (44%). In 1972-73, 35.1% of the St. Norbert freshmen left the school before becoming sophomores; 10 years later this figure decreased to 16.9%. A 1981 college survey found that 96.1% of St. Norbert graduates were successfully placed. Further, the endowment had increased to approximately $11 million by 1983 ($10 million over the 1973 figures), and total cash gifts had increased by $3 million. St. Norbert has a satisfied faculty, with a substantial development program and the second-highest wage scale among independent colleges in Wisconsin.

These accomplishments have been made possible, in part, by aggressive institutional advancement. St. Norbert has developed an extensive networking system and is quite sophisticated in the areas of public relations, marketing, and fund raising.

Most of St. Norbert's students come from Wisconsin and Illinois, and approximately three-fourths of them reside on campus. In 1982-83, 77% of them received financial aid. St. Norbert views a solid financial aid program as a cornerstone by which it can "attract the better students from all economic levels and maintain a St. Norbert education as a solid alternative for the quality student."

A new General Education Program aimed at providing all students with a core of skills, knowledge, and experience was implemented during the 1982-83 school year. Specifically, the goals of the program are to (1) make students aware of the Catholic Christian tradition and challenge them to identify their own moral and religious convictions; (2) foster the development of essential skills; (3) help students appreciate the importance of method in intellectual pursuits by experiencing the processes by which learning is accomplished in various disciplines; (4) help students develop an understanding of human nature, human relationships, and the natural world; (5) seek to help students achieve an awareness of the continuity and diversity of human experience; and (6) help students integrate knowledge from a variety of sources and to appreciate the relationship between ideas and experiences.

The success story of President Neil Webb testifies to the value of the basics in college management. He began with a carefully conceived plan. Next, he developed a sense of community and teamwork at the campus level by developing consensus on group goals. He then sought to build his executive team by locating the most talented people available. He paid these people top salaries and then gave them a high degree of autonomy in performing their duties. He nurtured total and open communications within this team by encouraging frequent inter-office visits and continual dialogue.

Neil Webb displayed a sound command of the fundamentals. He was a rational manager closely in tune with group and interpersonal dynamics and was uniquely human in his approach to administration. He was stable, quiet, and "low key." He never forgot the value of listening to intuition when hard decisions had to be made.

Under the leadership of Thomas A. Manion, who took over the presidency in 1983, St. Norbert is continuing to advance. The focus is now on fine-tuning the educational experience at the college. St. Norbert is no longer concerned with mere survival, as it was 10 years ago; the question now is "How can the college be even better?"

The University of Georgia

The University of Georgia, located in Athens, was the first state university in America. Although chartered in 1785, the university only existed on paper until 1801, when the first students arrived to study Latin, Greek, mathematics, debate, and natural history under Joseph Meigs, the college's president and single faculty member. Before it was forced to close during the Civil War, the University of Georgia had an enrollment of approximately 100 students. The institution reopened in 1866 to 300 students and was designated a land-grant institution in 1872. The University System of Georgia was established in 1931, designating the university's branch campuses as separate institutions. The University of Georgia rapidly became a major institution in the state; the capstone of Georgia's higher education system, it influences "the entire structure of education in the state by leading the pace of achievement and creating a climate of intellectual and cultural development for all units in the system."

The university views its position within the University of Georgia system in terms of its three-part mission: teaching, research, and public service. Teaching is the university's primary responsibility, as evidenced by the large number of degree programs offered: 2 associate degrees and 15 baccalaureates in more than 200 major fields, 22 master's degrees in 134 areas, four doctoral degrees in 84 areas, 40 specialist in education degree programs, and professional degree programs in accounting, forest resources, journalism, law, pharmacy, social work, and veterinary medicine. The university has 117 academic departments and 13 schools and colleges. Enrollment in the fall quarter of 1984 was 25,230 students.

The University of Georgia is among the nation's top 25 institutions in the number of National Merit and National Achievement scholars it enrolls. The University of Georgia counts among its alumni 22 governors of Georgia as well as many statesmen, military leaders, scientists, business leaders, educators, artists, and writers. Approximately 80% of the 1,800 faculty members hold the highest degree awarded in their field.

A commitment to basic and applied research in all academic disciplines characterizes the University of Georgia. Ranked among the nation's top 50 research universities, it spent more than $70 million on research in 1982-83, half of which came from research grants and contracts. The institution's total funding for research as of September 1984 exceeded $82 million; in five years the research budget has increased more than $28 million, with biotechnology and supercomputer technology currently constituting the major research thrusts.

The biological resources and biotechnology program was established in 1984 "to help university researchers meet the challenges of the developing revolution in biotechnological applications." Over 500 investigators are presently involved in research in botany, genetics, microbiology, veterinary medicine, and other bioscience areas, and the program supports about 20 postdoctoral appointments. The biotechnology program is a coordinated effort that the school hopes will attract biotechnology firms in search of university research support and allow research at the University of Georgia "to have a greater impact in food and fiber production, chemical feedstock production, and new energy sources and pharmaceutics also."

The University of Georgia's Advanced Computational Methods Center is a major initiative that places the university at the forefront in the development of high performance computer systems. ETA Systems, a supercomputer firm, decided in 1983 to locate its Advanced Programming Development Division at the University of Georgia to develop more powerful computers and to produce the software for the upcoming generation of supercomputers. The institution states that because of the presence of ETA and the subsequent acquisition of two powerful computers, a Cyber 205 advanced vector processor and a Cyberplus parallel architectural system, the University of Georgia will have "facilities unequalled in any other university in the nation for education, research, and collaboration with industry." The center has received large amounts of financial support from industry and state and federal-funding agencies.

Finally, the University of Georgia, as the state's land-grant institution, has a large and comprehensive program of public service. In each of Georgia's 159 counties, the Cooperative Extension Service provides extension programs in four areas: agriculture and natural resources, home economics, community and rural development, and youth development. The Georgia Center for Continuing Education serves over 100,000 annually for conferences, seminars, workshops, on- and off-campus credit and noncredit programs, and independent study in more than 3,000 educational programs. In 1984, the center received $7.2 million of an $8.4 million W. K. Kellogg Foundation grant awarded to the University of Georgia. With an additional allocation of $5.4 million from the state to renovate facilities, the Georgia Center for Continuing Education "will have an expanded role to play nationally in leadership development and programming for lifelong learning."

In 1982, President Davison announced nine goals that will be used to direct the course of the University of Georgia for a five-year period, goals identified from a university system state-wide needs assessment: (1) to continue the university's progress toward becoming a world center in the fields of production, conversion, processing, marketing, and distribution, both nationally and internationally, of biomass; (2) to insure that hard-earned national prominence in areas such as the natural and physical sciences is not eroded, in no way implying decreased support for other areas; (3) to remain attractive to the best Georgia high school graduates and maintain a suitable mix of students from out of state; (4) to insure that every graduate of the university has attained an acceptable level of computer knowledge; (5) to institutionalize more completely the university's relationships with the private sector, both in the small business and corporate areas; (6) to install and implement computing and other communications capabilities across the state so that all citizens can utilize the university's resources to improve their knowledge and productivity; (7) to continue to manage the university in the most cost-effective manner possible with the resources provided; (8) to continue to assess the economic climate and career opportunities in the state for the university's graduates and to modify the university's program to meet those needs; and (9) to maintain at a high level the quest for outside, private funding, based on the recognition that the university will remain a state-assisted institution and that the measure of its quality will depend in part on outside, private funding.

Publicizing its 200th year, the school noted that: "More than ever before, the University of Georgia is fulfilling its three missions—teaching, research and service." President Davison quotes

John Masefield, saying "Wherever a university stands, it stands and shines. Davison adds that "we can proudly say the University of Georgia's quality and performance rank it among the best."

University of Maryland System plus College Park Campus

The University of Maryland is located at the two ends of the Washington, D.C.-Baltimore corridor. Its major residential land grant campus is located at College Park, just outside the nation's capital, and two campuses—University of Maryland-Baltimore County (a smaller commuter campus) and University of Maryland in Baltimore (the medical-professional campus) are located in Maryland's largest city, Baltimore, a major East Coast seaport, Baltimore. The university has a fourth campus, the small historically black land grant, University of Maryland-Eastern Shore, plus a large nontraditional college, University College.

Maryland's history of support for higher education and the numerous attempts to establish a state university in Maryland are recounted by Malcolm Moos in *The Post-Land Grant University: The University of Maryland Report.* The state had considerable difficulty in putting its flagship university together: and, it was well into the twentieth century before the University of Maryland became recognized as a major state university.

The university, developed under the leadership of two educator presidents, Byrd and Elkins, was by the middle of the 1970s an average, or perhaps a slightly above average, primary state university. For decades it had suffered under two challenges: first, it shares Baltimore with a major national private research university (Johns Hopkins) and Washington with a cluster of national private universities (Georgetown, George Washington, and American University) which diverted attention and served to keep the pressure off Maryland to develop its state university. One result of this proximity to major private universities was an exaggeration of the importance of intercollegiate sports at College Park, both internally and externally. Secondly, the primary constituents of the University of Maryland until recent years were government employees living in the suburbs, a large state-wide farming industry, and the industrial port city of Baltimore. The concerns of many in these communities did not include building a university to be known nationally for its excellence. Access was more important.

The 1960s and 1970s changed all this as the Washington-Baltimore corridor became a high technology industrial mecca. High tech was changing the way the Pentagon did business, and the Nixon administration accelerated a process already underway—decreasing government employment by contracting with the private sector for services. Furthermore, biotechnology has become a dynamic growth industry, and having the National Institutes for Health in Bethesda is having a profound impact on suburban Maryland.

These changes are attracting national corporations to Maryland —IBM, Fairchild, Martin-Marietta, etc.—and home-grown high tech companies are popping up like weeds. Executives who are highly trained scientists and engineers are involved in these enterprises, and many moved from communities like San José or metropolitan Boston where there is a great wealth of excellent institutions of higher education. Community expectations began to rise and the University of Maryland began to get nervous.

Malcolm Moos, in *The Post-Land Grant University,* made the following observation, "The Baltimore-Washington corridor now has the highest concentration of highly trained technical, professional, and managerial workers in the nation."

Thus, when the University of Maryland board began its search for a successor to President Wilson Elkins in 1977, these things were considered. In choosing John S. Toll they found a scientist educator who was an established hardworking university president, and a man who wanted to move the university into a position of national recognition for excellence in teaching, research, and service.

Shortly after Toll took over the reins as president on July 1, 1978, he secured a $190,000 planning grant and commissioned Malcolm Moos to develop a plan for excellence for Maryland's state university. Moos's excellent report *The Post-Land Grant University* contained recommendations for both "new directions" and "strategies for excellence," both reflecting Toll's ambitions for the university.

While the Moos report is a good general road map, the real impetus to make Maryland a "top ten" public university seems to come from Toll's conceptual plan for the development of the university, which we believe he brought with him from SUNY-Stony Brook. Toll's plan, like most good strategic plans, is simple (but originally appeared to be beyond the reach of Maryland) and has two components: (1) elevating standards for appointments, promotions, and tenure for Maryland faculty to "top ten" standards; and (2) forging a dynamic relationship with Maryland's business community, including the high tech sector.

Toll implemented his plan immediately by rejecting many recommendations for tenure coming from the campuses in his first year. Initially there was a great hue and cry (especially from College Park) that the president was injecting himself into campus affairs in which he had no business. However, standards tightened all the way back to the departments. In recent years, Toll has approved far more recommendations than he has rejected. This mechanism has not only changed attitudes on campus but brought a greater appreciation for Maryland in places like Ann Arbor, Austin, Berkeley, and Charlottesville.

Although a more complex goal than upgrading faculty standards, Toll set about forming a partnership with business and industry in a very direct manner. His approach has included: a statewide graduate engineering program using interactive television; a cooperative program with one of Maryland's major employers, Fairchild Industries; creating a Maryland Science and Technology Center, and developing the Center for Advanced Research in Biotechnology, among others ventures.

The Maryland Science and Technology Center is actually a 465-acre campus-like research park that is being jointly developed by the university and private developers. The plan is to lure high tech research and manufacturing operations to this site by emphasizing the university's capabilities, the highly educated work force in the region, and its proximity to the nation'a capital. The project has already met with success as the Defense Advanced Research Programs Agency has selected the center as the location of a supercomputer research facility.

The Biotechnology Center is a joint endeavor of the university and the Commerce Department's National Bureau of Standards

(NBS). The two cooperating partners hope to attract researchers from industry and other organizations to the Shady Grove Life Sciences Center in Rockville.

Maryland is a large and diverse university, two characteristics that make change more difficult than it is for smaller institutions. However, it is clear to us that Maryland is beginning to change, as a result of two major factors; an evolving community with high expectations and a determined president.

The University of Tennessee, Knoxville

The University of Tennessee, Knoxville, (UTK) founded as Blount College in 1794 (two years before Tennessee became a state), was the first coeducational college in the nation. Today UTK is Tennessee's major comprehensive university and the only public institution in the state to encompass a full range of professional schools. It is also the state's major research institution, receiving about $25 million annually for funded research projects. Two major national institutions are within a 25-mile radius of UTK: the Oak Ridge National Laboratory (ORNL) and the headquarters of the Tennessee Valley Authority (TVA). The university has forged strong alliances, including the UT/ORNL Distinguished Scientist Program and the new computer system connecting the university's network to the Oak Ridge network and providing UTK users with access to the data bases ORNL shares with other federal laboratories. The University of Tennessee, Knoxville enjoys providing educational services to the community and they in turn enjoy strong public support of the institution.

The immediate setting of the university is urban, with three interstate highways and an airport close to campus, but the forests of East Tennessee and the Great Smoky Mountains National Park are a short drive from the university. Knoxville has been rated one of the "most livable" places in the nation by the Rand McNally *Places Rated Almanac*. It is clear that both faculty and administration believe that the university contributes to, as well as benefits from, the quality of life that earned Knoxville its rating. There is a strong sense of pride and institutional identity among students, faculty, and staff at UTK. In 1984 the *College Money Book* stated that the Knoxville campus is the Volunteer State's "best buy" for students, based on "high quality education at an economical cost."

"The Hill," as the original campus is known, is only a small part of the 417-acre complex, the oldest and largest campus of the university. In addition to the Knoxville facilities, UTK has off-campus centers in Tullahoma (UT Space Institute), Kingsport, and Oak Ridge, and branches of the School of Social Work in Knoxville, Nashville, and Memphis. Some 25,000 students from all 50 states and 90 foreign countries are enrolled at UTK.

The university's mission has changed recently to focus more on national issues, and to become more selective. The university deliberately reduced enrollment from 30,000 in 1984 to 25,000 in the fall of 1985, with negotiated assistance from the state in protecting the institution from financial penalty. It also initiated, for the first time in its history, selective admissions. The new admission criteria are designed to preserve broad access to the institution but to encourage students who do not exhibit a reasonable chance of academic success to seek remedial help elsewhere, for example at one of the 10 community colleges in the state.

There is a broad consensus on the goals and mission of the university. Chancellor Jack Reese has written about the mission as follows:

> In formulating a fresh strategic mission for the university, our emphasis must continue to be basic research, even while we reach out to strengthen our alliances with the public and private sectors. Our own particular strength, like that of all research universities (where 60% of the nation's research takes place), is the ability to investigate freely; to spin out promising ideas without the pressure to develop products; to build upon the base of information and knowledge in ways that increase mankind's storehouse of understanding. . . . In this tradition the university seeks to uphold while at the same time creating new pathways for the application of research in both the public and private sectors. . . . The university is also enlarging its vision and refining the mechanisms to carry out its new regional and national role.

According to Reese, "UTK has long been an academic power in the Tennessee Valley. It is now bidding to become a national power as we develop a model for merging scientific and technical resources with academic, industrial and governmental strength."

Reese sums up the general ambitions of UTK by saying that they are intended to "improve the quality of the university and to enhance its image and reputation." The quest for quality is a driving force of the institution. The quality of the faculty has been cited by a recent publication as being "largely responsible for the outstanding academic reputation the university enjoys." One case in point is Dr. William Bass, head of the Anthropology Department, who has been a major factor in guiding UTK forensic anthropology department to national recognition. Bass has been named 1985 national professor of the year by the Council for Advancement and Support of Education (CASE). Carnegie Foundation president, Ernest Boyer, describes Bass as "committed to excellence in the lecture hall and the laboratory."

Some other ways in which quality is enhanced at UTK are curriculum revision, strategic planning, improved advising, expanding exchange programs, and obtaining increased private support. The University has in place, for the first time in its history, an effective strategic planning process under the direction of the Provost and the Executive Vice Chancellor for Business, Planning, and Finance. Comprehensive academic program reviews, student outcome assessments, and other evaluative techniques are being used to improve the quality of programs and services. Conversion from a quarter to a semester calendar is being planned and will be effective in the fall term of 1988. This transition is intended to reemphasize the general education "core" of all curricula and to encourage rigorous examination of priorities and focusing of resources by the various departments and colleges.

The increased emphasis of the state on quality public education has been a major opportunity of which the university has taken advantage. "Things seem to have come together all at one time," noted one administrator, "and Tennessee has taken advantage of this." Another commented, "We are in a special moment in time, and we must grasp the opportunity."

The University of Tennessee, Knoxville has been much assisted by improved funding from the state which has occurred in the last two years and which is the result of comprehensive education reform legislation. Of particular significance are the "Centers of Excellence" and the "Chairs of Excellence," funded by a combination of state and private/grant and contract support. The Chairs of Excellence program was established to provide "increased student access to Tennessee's very best faculty members." The University of Tennessee, Knoxville is one of 10 state institutions participating in this program.

Asked to comment on the university's accomplishments, Reese said:

> I believe that we have accomplished what we have primarily because we have decided what the university is and is not. We have decided on a specific course of action which suits our history and location, which reflects our assets and liabilities, and which is based on a realistic notion of how much we can do over specific periods of time. Above all, we have established our identitiy. Each college and university is much like each other, but each is significantly different. We have determined the culture and personality and mission of this university and are intent on projecting an accurate and honest image of ourselves.
>
> My recent tasks have been to set a tone, establish an attitude, build consensus within and outside the university about change and direction, encourage teamwork, and advertise the university. What is happening is very much the result of many people working together.

The University of Tulsa

The University of Tulsa began in 1894 at Muskogee, Oklahoma, as Henry Kendall College. The College moved to Tulsa, in 1907, and 14 years later became the University of Tulsa. A private Presbyterian-affiliated institution, the University of Tulsa has a total enrollment of approximately 5,500 men and women, 1,500 of whom are enrolled in graduate programs. The student-teacher ratio is 15 to 1, and the 1984 freshman class enrolled 55 National Merit Scholars. The University has 10 endowed chairs—each supported by $1 million. Six undergraduate degrees are offered in 80 academic areas and 25 graduate programs include doctoral degrees in education, English, engineering, geosciences, and industrial/organizational psychology.

Although the traditional goal of the University of Tulsa has been to provide a quality liberal education to its students, the institution began a new era when J. Paschal Twyman assumed the presidency in 1968. Under Twyman's administration the school blossomed and building activity and funds began to grow rapidly. In the late 1970s, President Twyman initiated the largest capital campaign in the history of the institution, "Dimensions for a New Decade." This campaign, which sought to raise $43 million, began during a period of declining enrollments and escalating costs for the private sector. Although the University of Tulsa was stable in the early 1970s (thanks to successful fund raising), President Twyman and the trustees realized that an even stronger financial base was needed to move forward in the 1980s.

After three years of strategic planning, the "Decade" campaign began in October 1978, with $25 million already given or pledged. A supportive Board of Trustees, as well as civic leaders, pushed the campaign's total over $50 million in just 18 months.

Five primary support areas were designated for these funds: academic enrichment, campus consolidation, library acquisitions, university endowment, and capital projects. The operating budget expanded, capital improvements reached $28 million, and $17 million was added to the endowment, which currently ranks in the top 1% in the nation.

A new core curriculum, based on the humanities and stressing interdisciplinary studies, was introduced in the College of Arts and Sciences in 1981. A major part of that curriculum, a nine-hour writing requirement, was soon implemented for all undergraduates at Tulsa. In 1983, a $300,000 grant from the National Endowment for the Humanities helped to fund the university-wide "Tulsa Curriculum," which aspires to be a national model for undergraduate education.

The Tulsa Curriculum is based on the belief that every Tulsa graduate should (1) possess certain intellectural skills essential to function in contemporary society; (2) acquire breadth of knowledge in several areas; and (3) pursue depth in a major subject. The Tulsa Curriculum provides "form and substance to the simultaneous development of intellectual skills and breadth of knowledge while students' college and major programs address proficiency in a particular subject." Regarded as the "common academic experience that characterizes all our students," the Tulsa Curriculum is composed of two parts, the core curriculum and the general curriculum. The core curriculum develops intellectual skills, and all students are required to complete three writing courses, demonstrate computer literacy, and complete the degree requirements specified by the student's college. The general curriculum develops breadth of knowledge by requiring each student to complete at least 27 hours of course work arranged into categories or blocks that "address broad intellectual concerns rather than traditional disciplinary clusters," course blocks such as "Human Imagination," "Human Institutions," "World Cultures," and "Contemporary Experience." The blocks change each term so that students are able to select from many courses. Tulsa also continues to expand its graduate programs. A Ph.D. in industrial/organizational psychology has been recently added. Other Ph.D.s are being planned in educational administration, mechanical engineering, and electrical/computer science.

As Tulsa continues to emphasize teaching and research, its reputation for academic excellence grows. As President Twyman noted, "Success means higher goals, and we are defining new goals now." The university plans to increase the number of enrolled National Merit Scholars to 100 by 1986, and there are plans to raise the trust and endowment funds from the present $170 million to $225 million by 1990. The University of Tulsa is well on its way to reaching its goal of providing strong undergraduate and graduate programs for a carefully selected clientele.

Paschal Twyman has a straightforward, buisness-like approach to leadership. First, in recruiting staff, he attempts "to find the strongest talent available." Because he has clearly defined those administrative areas for which he is responsible (i.e., community/public relations; development); everything else is then delegated to his executive team. Once his expectations are made known, his staff is given a high degree of autonomy, "almost to the point of neglect." He trusts his staff to do their jobs. Performance is rewarded; incompetence is punished.

President Twyman believes universities are responsible for contributing to both the preservation of our society and to the development of new and innovative thought. He asserts an autonomous university is the only way to best serve society and innovation. When political and sectarian alliances are formed, there is an automatic assumption of the inherent deficiencies and limitations of both entities.

Appendix A: Nominated Institutions

These colleges and universities were nominated in our survey of higher education experts:

Aims Community College (Colorado)

Alverno (Wisconsin)

Arkansas, University of (Arkansas)

Aquinas College (Michigan)

Bard College (New York)

Bethany College (Kansas)

Birmingham Southern College (Alabama)

Bradford College (Massachusetts)

Bronx Community College (New York)

Buena Vista College (Iowa)

California State University (San Diego)

Carleton College (Minnesota)

Carnegie Mellon (Pennsylvania)

Central College (Iowa)

Central Florida, University of (Florida)

Chicago State University (Illinois)

Claremont McKenna College (California)

Clayton Jr. College (Georgia)

Colorado College (Colorado)

Dallas Community College (Texas)

DePaul University (Illinois)

District of Columbia, University of

DuPage, College of (Illinois)

Eastern Michigan University (Michigan)

Eastern Oregon State (Oregon)

Georgia State University (Georgia)

Georgia, University of (Georgia)

Gettysburg College (Pennsylvania)

Goddard College (Vermont)

Gonzaga University (Washington)

Hartford, University of (Connecticut)

High Point College (North Carolina)

Hood College (Maryland)

Indiana University (Indiana)

Kennesaw College (Georgia)

Lane Community College (Oregon)

Louisville, University of (Kentucky)

Maricopa Community College District (Arizona)

Maryland, University of (Maryland)

Marylhurst College (Oregon)

Marymount Manhattan College (New York)

Memphis State University (Tennessee)

Miami Dade Community College (Florida)

Miami, University of (Florida)

Millsaps College (Mississippi)

Minnesota, University of, Morris (Minnesota)

Mira Costa Community College (California)

Mississippi, University of (Mississippi)

New York, State University of (New York)

Albany

Binghamtom

Brockport

Canton

Delhi

New Paltz

Oswego

Potsdam

Utica

Nebraska, University of (Nebraska)

North Carolina, University of, Charlotte (North Carolina)

Northeast Missouri State University (Missouri)

Northern Arizona University (Arizona)

Northwestern University (Illinois)

Oakland University (Michigan)

Oakwood College (Alabama)

Pennsylvania, University of (Pennsylvania)

Purdue University (Indiana)

Philadelphia Community College (Pennsylvania)

Portland Community College (Oregon)

Queens College (North Carolina)

Rensselaer Polytechnic Institute (New York)

Richmond, University of (Virginia)

St. John's University (Minnesota)

St. Mary's College (Kansas)

St. Norbert College (Wisconsin)

San Francisco, University of (California)

Smith College (Massachusetts)

South Carolina, University of (South Carolina)

Spelman College (Georgia)

Stanford University (California)

Stephens College (Massachusetts)

Stillman College (Alabama)

Tennessee Technical University (Tennessee)

Tennessee, University of (Tennessee)

Texas, University of, Austin (Texas)

Thomas Edison State College (New Jersey)

Towson State University (Maryland)

Trenton State University (New Jersey)

Trinity University (Texas)

Triton Community College (Illinois)

Tulsa, University of (Oklahoma)

Washington and Lee (Virginia)

Wilson College (Pennsylvania)

Whitman College (Washington)

Wisconsin, University of (Wisconsin)

Appendix B: Interview Questionnaire

I. Introduction: Your institution has been nominated to be part of a national study of aggressively advancing colleges. Background given as needed.

II. Institutional Assessment
1. What do you consider to be the driving forces at your college?
   Motivations?
   Unique educational vision?
2. How would you characterize the personality of your institution?
3. What is the institutional climate like here?
4. What initiatives or undertakings have you begun which would illustrate your college is truly on the move?
   How did this all start? Who was involved? Why?
   Was this a high risk?
   Any obstacles in getting this going? How did you pay for this?
   How's it going? Doing as it's supposed to? Unexpected outcomes?
   Has it affected the entire college?
   What do people think of it?
   Is there someone else we ought to speak with about this?
   Repeat for other initiatives

III. Regarding management and administration of the institution:
1. Is there anything distinctive about the managerial system of the college?
2. Are there any bottlenecks or stumbling blocks that impede progress?

IV. Leadership Assessment: Mention confidentiality is assured!
1. How would you describe the president's leadership or managerial style?

2. Can you give some examples of this style?
3. What does the president take pride in?
4. Characteristics check-off—as follows:

Leadership Assessment

The following statements relate to your president's leadership style. If you believe any descriptor applies, please say "yes," otherwise, say "no." Of course, you need not answer if you don't know.

	Strongly Disagree	Disagree	Don't Know	Agree	Strongly Agree
1. Visionary	___	___	___	___	___
2. Mediator	___	___	___	___	___
3. Innovative	___	___	___	___	___
4. A "by the book" manager (number oriented; strong on "chain of command")	___	___	___	___	___
5. A team builder (brings people into the process; identifies and motivates talented people)	___	___	___	___	___
6. Good at public relations (external and internal)	___	___	___	___	___
7. Delegates well	___	___	___	___	___
8. Opportunity conscious	___	___	___	___	___
9. Good at political affairs (state and local)	___	___	___	___	___
10. A good communicator	___	___	___	___	___
11. Authoritarian	___	___	___	___	___

12. Visible on
    campus   _____   _____   _____ _____ _____
13. Risk taker   _____   _____   _____ _____ _____
14. Good at shifting
    resources for new
    undertakings   _____   _____   _____ _____ _____
15. Controversial   _____   _____   _____ _____ _____
16. Encourages ideas;
    is receptive   _____   _____   _____ _____ _____
17. Pragmatic   _____   _____   _____ _____ _____
18. Optional: Com-
    passionate   _____   _____   _____ _____ _____

V. In conclusion:
    1. Has your institution changed much over the years?
    2. Where do you see the college going in the years ahead?
    3. Other people we have seen or will be seeing. Could you suggest
        others?

Appendix C: Survey of Institutional Initiatives

One important criterion used to select the 30 institutions "on-the-move" was their educational innovations or initiatives. In collecting specific information on the various institutions, the initiatives were catalogued by institution and by function, such as: relationships with business, technology and telecommunications, inter-institutional cooperation, general education, institutional recovery programs, physical plant, continuing education, curriculum innovation, mission refinement, marketing, public policy, and administrative policy and organization. A detailed list of the innovations/initiatives is presented in this section under the following 12 headings.

Initiatives

I. *RELATIONSHIP WITH BUSINESS*

1.	Carnegie-Mellon University	Extensive involvement with business
2.	Community College of Philadelphia	Linkage with business community
3.	Dallas County Community College	Business and industry task force
4.	College of DuPage	Business and Professional Institute
5.	Eastern Oregon State College	Direct service to business, private industry, and government agencies

6. George Mason University	George Mason Institute
7. High Point College	Linkage with furniture industry
8. Kennesaw College	Small Business Development Center
9. Portland Community College	Small Business Assistance Center, workshops, seminars, consulting and contracting programs
10. Queens College	Linkage with business and industry
11. Rensselaer Polytechnic Institute	Extensive involvement with industry, for example, Center for Industrial Innovation
12. Stanford University	Extensive involvement with business and industry
13. University of Central Florida	Plans for Central Florida Research Park
14. University of Maryland	Cooperative ventures with business and industry
15. University of North Carolina, Charlotte	Development of University Place, University City, and University Research Park
16. University of Texas	Linkage with business as institution attempts to develop world class research and education programs

II. TECHNOLOGY AND TELECOMMUNICATIONS

1. Aims Community College	Substantial commitment to use of information technology in teaching
2. Carnegie-Mellon University	Emphasis on computers and technology
3. Dallas County Community College	Exemplary telecommunications system
4. DuPage College	Delivery system includes telecourses, radio, and cable television
5. George Mason University	George Mason Institute

6. Kansas State University	Landon Lecture Series which promote a national visibility for science and technology
7. Lane Community College	Substantial commitment to information technologies in instruction
8. Maricopa Community College	High Technology Advisory Council; emphasis on high technology and computerization; telephone courses for the handicapped
9. Miami-Dade Community College	Expertise in producing complete media instructional packages through its Life Lab Program
10. Northern Virginia Community College	Extended Learning Institute, which provides television and radio courses, and audio and video cassettes for independent study; project to develop a communications network of all Virginia cable systems which are to be used for instruction
11. Portland Community College	Instructional delivery system includes cable and broadcast television and telecommunications satellite system; commitment to utilize technology in every program
12. Rensselaer Polytechnic Institute	Center for Industrial Innovation; Center for Rotocraft Technology
13. Stanford University	Center for Integrated Systems; Center for Biotechnology Research; Linear Accelerator Center, etc.
14. University of Central Florida	High technology tenets are the nucleus of a symbiotic relationship between applied science and university researchers; commitment to use of technology

15. University of Georgia	Research in biotechnology and supercomputer technology; Advanced Computational Methods Center
16. University of Texas	Commitment to developing world class research and education programs in microelectronics, electrical engineering, computer engineering, and computer science

III. *INTER-INSTITUTIONAL COOPERATION*

1. Stillman College	Entered into cooperative arrangement with neighboring University of Alabama
2. SUNY Agricultural and Technical College at Canton	Cooperation with St. Lawrence University and Clarkson College of Technology
3. SUNY Potsdam	Cooperation with neighboring St. Lawrence University and Clarkson College of Technology
4. St. Mary's College	Cooperative ventures with area community colleges

IV. *GENERAL EDUCATION*

1. Alverno College	Ability based developmentally oriented curriculum
2. Bradford College	Bradford Plan for a Practical Liberal Arts Education
3. Clayton Junior College	Outcome-focused, assessment-based general education program
4. George Mason University	Plan for Alternative General Education
5. Goddard College	Education for Practical Idealist
6. University of Tennessee-Knoxville	Value added type program

V. *FACULTY/STAFF DEVELOPMENT*

1. Dallas County Community College	Career development and renewal plan; Wonderful Wednesday

	Program; Uncommittee, a monthly literature discussion among colleagues
2. Lane Community College	Quality Circles Program where employees meet regularly to discuss problems of quality in their work areas
3. Maricopa Community College	Emphasis on faculty and staff development; retraining programs
4. University of Texas	Enhanced faculty through recruitment of outstanding scholars throughout country, 703 endowed faculty positions
5. College of DuPage	President's Risk Fund for innovative projects

VI. *INSTITUTIONAL RECOVERY*

1. Bradford College
2. Goddard College
3. Marylhurst College of Lifelong Learning
4. Queens College
5. St. Norbert College
6. Wilson College

VII. *PHYSICAL PLANT*

1. Aims Community College	Major expansion of campus facilities
2. Rensselaer Polytechnic Institute	Construction of Center for Industrial Innovation
3. Stillman College	Instituted successful campus beautification program
4. SUNY College of Technology at Utica-Rome	Extensive building program
5. University of Georgia	Construction of Center for Continuing Education
6. University of Hartford	New buildings and dorms
7. University of Maryland	Campus beautification program

8. Lane Community College — Energy Management Program

VIII. *CONTINUING EDUCATION*

1. Alverno College — Weekend College
2. Aquinas College — Easttown Project; Emeritus College; fully age integrated
3. Community College of Philadelphia — Outreach programs for neighborhood
4. DePaul University — School for New Learning
5. College of DuPage — Programs for specific target groups including senior citizens, women, and children
6. Eastern Oregon State College — External degree programs
7. Thomas Edison State College — External degree institution
8. Hood College — Emphasis on nontraditional students
9. Kansas State University — Off-campus education including outreach credit classes, nontraditional study, the Regents' Network, noncredit training for business and industry, and conferences at the national, regional, and local levels
10. Kennesaw College — Center for Excellence in Teaching and Learning, a joint venture between the college, county, and city school systems to serve instructional and professional needs of public school teachers
11. Maricopa Community College — Open College
12. Marylhurst College — First accredited degree-granting institution in nation devoted to lifelong learning and granting college credit for lifelong learning
13. Memphis State University — Alcohol and drug abuse services provide linkage between university and the state

14. Northern Virginia Community College	Extended Learning Institute
15. Queens College	Four new programs for adults; new college undergraduate liberal arts program for part-time students
16. Saint Mary's College	Aggressive outreach to adult populations
17. University of Georgia	Georgia Center for Continuing Education; National Center for Leadership Development in Adult and Continuing Education and Lifelong Learning
18 University of Tennessee	Plans to orient more programs to adults

IX. *CURRICULUM*

1. Alverno College	Ability based curriculum
2. Bradford College	Plan for the practical liberal arts
3. Bronx Community College	Improvement of academic atmosphere
4. Colorado College	Block Plan represents a novel method of scheduling
5. DePaul University	Management Fellows Program that combines the liberal arts with a semester long paid internship with a Fortune 500 company; one of the factors contributing to a 30% increase in applications
6. George Mason University	Emphasis on providing an excellent undergraduate liberal arts education
7. Maricopa Community College	Comprehensive program evaluation
8. Millsaps College	Curricular changes to strengthen student development orientation
7. Mira Costa College	Freshman English courses require students to demonstrate exit-level proficiency which is common of all students; courses in

	computer-assisted drafting; biology field studies; computer arts/music program
8. Northwest Missouri State University	Curriculum has a value-added measure of evaluation; strong commitment to effective writing skills
9. Rensselaer Polytechnic Institute	Technical writing program; academic-base program in robotics
10. SUNY Binghamton	Substantial new engineering initiatives
11. SUNY New Paltz	New initiatives in engineering
12. SUNY Oswego	Increased emphasis on writing skills and foreign languages; extensive review of curriculum
13. University of Central Florida	Offers new Ph.D. program in computer science

X. *Mission*

1. Community College of Philadelphia	Examination of college's philosophical foundation coupled with a plan for excellence
2. Eastern Oregon State College	Mission was drastically revised to provide services to a larger geographic area
3. Northern Arizona Community College	Redefined mission in a rural setting via targeted undergraduate programs offered through outreach programs throughout the state
4. SUNY College of Technology at Utica-Rome	Major refocus of mission

XI. *MARKETING*

1. Carleton College	Implemented a strategic marketing plan to identify its "natural constituency" which has resulted in increased applicant pool

2. Eastern Oregon State College	Improved marketing strategy
3. Marylhurst College of Lifelong Learning	Vigorous advertising and publicity campaign
4. Oakwood College	Massive recruitment drive in Egypt, Africa, and Caribbean
5. Rensselaer Polytechnic Institute	Aggressive fund-raising strategy
6. Saint Norbert College	Used students, parents, and counselors to network Chicago area with message of excellence
7. SUNY Agricultural and Technical College at Delhi	Aggressive student recruiting
8. University of Hartford	Aggressive advertising
9. University of Miami	Improve publications and fund raising
10. University of Texas	Marketing Plan to recruit top talent

XII. *PUBLIC POLICY*

1. George Mason University	Emphasis on public policy
2. Kennesaw College	Institute for Public and Social Services; endowed Chair of Public Enterprise
3. SUNY Albany	New initiatives in public policy programs
4. University of Wisconsin	LaFollette Institute for Government Affairs

XIII. *ADMINISTRATIVE POLICY AND ORGANIZATION*

1. Clayton Junior College	Comprehensive academic reorganization in which schools and departments were created to replace divisions
2. Miami-Dade Community College	New management system and redefinition of faculty roles
3. SUNY Binghamton	Well-coordinated planning process

4. University of Hartford	Better faculty and deans
5. University of Maryland	Completed major self-study
6. University of Miami	Bold strategic plan including refined administrative structure
7. University of Pennsylvania	Major change in financial aid practices
8. University of Tennessee	Reduction in enrollment

Bibliography

Bibliography

BELL, DANIEL. *The Coming of the Post-Industrial Society.* New York: Basic Books, 1973.

BOTKIN, JAMES, ET AL. *Global Stakes.* New York: Harper & Row, 1982.

CAREY, WILLIAM. "The Elegance of Choosing." *Science,* December 21, 1984.

CLARK, BURTON R. *The Distinctive College: Antioch, Reed & Swarthmore.* Chicago: Aldine, 1970.

COHEN, MICHAEL D., AND MARCH, JAMES G. *Leadership and Ambiguity: The American College President.* New York: McGraw-Hill, 1974.

COMMISSION ON STRENGTHENING PRESIDENTIAL LEADERSHIP, ASSOCIATION OF GOVERNING BOARDS OF UNIVERSITIES AND COLLEGES. *Presidents Make a Difference: Strengthening Leadership in Colleges and Universities.* (Directed by Clark Kerr). Washington, D. C., 1984.

DE TOQUEVILLE, ALEXIS. *Democracy in America.* A new translation by George Lawrence. New York: Harper & Row, 1966.

DRUCKER, PETER F. *Technology, Management and Society: Essays.* New York: Harper & Row, 1970.

GODWIN, WINFRED L. "Foreword." In James R. Mingle and Associates: *Challenges of Retrenchment.* San Francisco: Jossey-Bass, 1981.

JOHNSTON, DAVID. "Reports: The Resurrection of Marylhurst." *Change,* December/January, 1979.

KELLER, GEORGE. *Academic Strategy: The Management Revolution in American Higher Education.* Baltimore: Johns Hopkins University Press, 1983.

KERR, CLARK. "Leadership Begins with Your President." *AGB Reports,* January/February, 1985.

NAISBITT, JOHN. *Megatrends: Ten New Directions Transforming Our Lives.* New York: Warner Books, 1982.

PECK, ROBERT D. "Entrepreneurship and Small College Leadership." 1983.

PETERS, THOMAS J., AND WATERMAN, ROBERT H., JR. *In Search of Excellence: Lessons from America's Best Run Companies.* New York: Harper & Row, 1982.

SCHOENBERG, ROBERT. *Geneen.* New York: Norton, 1985.

Index